DIVORCED DAD'S HANDBOOK   3

This book is dedicated to
Rozanne, Evan & Tasha
& Karen

CONTENTS ━━━━

DIVORCED DAD'S HANDBOOK

100 QUESTIONS & ANSWERS

by Robert Bernstein and Richard Worth

DIVORCED DAD'S HANDBOOK

BLUE BIRD PUBLISHING
1739 East Broadway #306
Tempe AZ 85202
(602) 968-4088 (602) 831-6063

ISBN 0-933025-40-8 $12.95
Cover Art by Richard Rossiter

Library of Congress Cataloguing in Publication Data

Bernstein, Robert, 1945-
    Divorced dad's handbook : 100 questions and answers/
by Robert Bernstein and Richard Worth.
    p.   cm.
    Includes bibliographical references.
    ISBN 0-933025-40-8 (pbk.)
    1. Divorce fathers--Psychology. 2. Divorced fathers--Family
relationships. 3. Children of divorced parents.   I. Worth,
Richard. II. Title.
HQ756.B465   1995
306.85'6--dc20
                                          95-21436
                                            CIP

How do you control your anger?
How do you work on accepting the change in your life?
How can you begin to develop more satisfying adult
   relationships in the future?

How do you find the right attorney?
What questions should you ask to evaluate an attorney?
What should you expect to pay for a divorce?
What information will your lawyer need from you?
What is discovery?
Why are your expectations of your attorney important?
How can you work with your lawyer most effectively?
When should you change lawyers?
Should you hire a "cutthroat" lawyer?
How long should the divorce process last?
What is "fair" in terms of spousal support and child support?
What happens if you don't pay your support payments?
Should you try to settle your divorce without going to trial?
Is our adversarial legal system the best way to deal with
   divorce cases?
What is mediation?
When should you consider mediation?
What is the cost of mediation?
How do you find an effective mediator?
What happens in the mediation process?
Are there cases that should not be submitted to mediation?
What types of custody arrangements are common in divorce
   cases?
Can a divorce agreement be changed?

What kind of visitation schedule should you try to achieve?
Can you change a visitation schedule?
What should you do if your former wife wants to reduce your
   visitation schedule?

What should you do if this woman and your children do not get
along well?
What role should this woman play with your children?
How do you strike a balance in your relationships with a
woman and your children?
How do you deal with sexual intimacy around your children?
What feelings can you expect to experience if your ex-
wife becomes involved with another man or remarries?
How do you cope with the fear of being displaced in your
children's lives by another man?
What attitude should you have toward this new man in your
wife's life?

If your ex-wife prevents you from seeing your children during
visitations, should you ever consider running off with
them?
Can the police ever assist you in enforcing your visitation
schedule?
Should you ever consider withholding child support payments?
Can the amount of child support you're paying ever be
reduced?
How else can you appeal to your ex-wife to resolve the conflict
between you?
What can your lawyer do to assist you?
How can you help your lawyer with the case?
Should you represent yourself in court?
Should you file for custody of your children to put leverage on
your ex-wife?

INTRODUCTION: Where Do I Go From Here?

Popular belief has it that men are just too indifferent or self-centered to maintain a meaningful relationship with their children following a divorce. The stereotype of a divorced father is a man indulging himself in every imaginable type of hedonistic excess, or the Deadbeat Dad who skips town to avoid paying his child support. Unfortunately, statistics seem to bear out these stereotypes. Forty percent of all children report rarely seeing their fathers following a divorce. And even for the one child in six who is fortunate enough to see his Dad once a week, it may seem more like a visit from Santa Claus than a true parent-child relationship.

What happens to so many fathers after a divorce? Are they content to simply slam the door on one segment of their lives and coldly turn their backs on family responsibilities, as the media would often have us believe? Are they incapable of being real parents? Or is the reality far more complicated? We think it is. Many men, we believe, want a satisfying relationship with their children—some are even achieving it—but they must often overcome formidable obstacles that stand in the way.

Divorce alienates men from their own families. It's an embarrassment, a magnified sense of failure, which produces pain, anger and loss of control. Some of the divorced men interviewed for this book told us that they believed their children were being "held hostage" for child support payments. And even if they paid regularly and on time, the men still felt that their ex-wives might withhold the children—as some did—on a sheer whim to prevent their fathers from seeing them for visitations. For many men, the visitation period—limited as it is—makes them feel like part-time fathers, unable to have a significant impact on their children. Studies show that men who were deeply involved in the lives of their children prior to a divorce have an unusually difficult time adjusting to being divorced Dads. As one father explained, every time he had to drop off his children after they had spent a weekend together, it brought tears to his eyes.

As a result, some men decide to escape. They accept a new job out of state or marry the first woman who shows an interest in them and try to begin a new life with her. But by leaving their children behind, these men are often doing irreparable damage to them.

Research shows that divorce can have a substantial long-term negative effect on children, undermining such things as their achievement in school and their ability to form lasting relationships. Nevertheless, this impact can be mitigated if divorced parents will somehow set aside their own problems for the sake of the children and the divorced Dads can remain a significant presence in their lives.

This book has been written for men who want to continue to be involved with their children following a divorce but may not know exactly how to do it successfully. Therefore, we have begun the book with a chapter that focuses on those issues that arise when a divorce occurs, such as when to tell the children, what to tell them, how to deal with reactions like sadness and insecurity, and how to reassure them that you will still play an important role in their lives. Chapter II looks at emotions you may be experiencing after the divorce and how to cope with them effectively. In Chapter III, we examine the numerous legal questions surrounding divorce, such as custody arrangements and child support, and discuss the pros and cons of mediation. The topic of Chapter IV is visitations—how to prepare for them, how to prevent them from becoming a battleground with your ex-wife, and what to do if she prevents you from seeing your kids. Men often have trouble bonding with their children follow-ing a divorce, and Chapter V presents a variety of topics around this all-important issue. In Chapter VI we describe some of the problems involved in raising children, especially the difficulties of communicating with your ex-wife so that both of you can provide a consistent approach to discipline, homework, chores and other important matters that pertain to child rearing. Chapters VII and VIII deal with the transformation in your children as they enter adolescence as well as the change in your own lifestyle as you develop an intimate relationship with a woman who may begin to play a significant role in the lives of your kids. (Many chapters contain a section at the end titled Letters with examples of how to communicate with your ex-wife and your children when you are not with them.)

Throughout the book, we emphasize repeatedly the im-portance of keeping open the lines of communication with your ex-wife and remaining as civil to her as possible for the sake of your children. Unfortunately, many men fall into the flight-or fight syndrome—either dropping out and abandoning their children, as we mentioned before, or allowing themselves to be easily provoked by their ex-wives and doing battle with them over every issue. Neither of these approaches benefits your kids. Instead, we suggest a variety of measures that will help you coexist relatively peacefully with your former wife—a skill which is critically important to being a successful divorced Dad.

Nevertheless, we also recognize that some situations cannot be easily resolved through communication. Therefore, in the final chapter of the book, If All Else Fails, we provide some suggestions to guide you in coping with those problems that may seem intractable.

As the title of our book suggests, it is written in an easy question-and-answer format because our experience talking with men is that they want practical solutions to immediate problems and don't want to wade through pages and pages of material to find the information they need. The book is based on hundreds of conversations with divorced men, as well as interviews with psychologists, social workers, divorce lawyers and mediators.

The book's co-authors come from different backgrounds. Bob Bernstein is a divorced father who has retained a close relationship with his two children over the decade following a divorce. As a former director of Big Brothers/Big Sisters, Bob saw many children who were victims of divorce—children who lived with a single parent (usually their mother) and desperately needed a father. This continuing problem, combined with the searing experience of his own divorce, convinced Bob to begin a support group for divorced Dads. He helped educate these

Dads and gave them the practical skills they needed to share their lives with their children.

Bob talked about the support group and his experiences as a divorced father on the NBC *Today* show. In addition, he was part of a small advocacy group that was instrumental in persuading the Connecticut Legislature to pass a law requiring divorcing parents with children to attend parent education classes.

Richard Worth is a professional writer, who has published nine books—two of them in the area of family living. He is currently writing a book for managers on leading the change process in large organizations. In addition, he is a media producer who creates corporate video presentations as well as documentaries on topics ranging from diversity in education to an eight-part radio series on Fiorello LaGuardia that aired on National Public Radio.

Like any book, this one could not have been completed without the assistance of a number of people. We wish to thank Karen Jeffers, Esq., Linda Mariani, Esq., and Brian LeClair, Esq.; Josephine Beebe, PhD., Barbara Rucci, MSW, Maxine Varenko, MS, and Andersen Williams, MSW; divorce mediators Robert Singer, PhD. and Anne Endyke, Esq.; and William Donovan, who hosts a television program for divorced fathers; as well as all the Dads who agreed to talk to us. These men spoke for divorced Dads everywhere who are trying to do what it takes to be good parents.

CHAPTER I

THE TUMULT OF DIVORCE

The early days of a divorce are surely among the most tumultuous in any man's life. "I had a hole right where my stomach was supposed to be," one man explained. "I had to take things one day at a time; it was too depressing to look any further ahead." As another man put it, when he left his home for the last time: "I felt empty—my kids weren't going to be there when I woke up in the morning. I wasn't going to be able to get them ready for bed or read them bedtime stories."

Divorce marks a watershed—a traumatic transition point—when a man leaves behind a home, a wife, an entire way of life, when he closes the door on broken dreams and promises to start over again. Change is always difficult, but especially so when the change is as wrenching as divorce for it forces a man to assume some unfamiliar and very uncomfortable roles. For example, he will become a visiting parent (for women generally become the custodial parents in divorce cases) whose activities with his children will now be shoehorned into a very tight and limiting schedule. He will often be called upon to support two homes: one where he used to live but now enters only as an unwelcome guest, and another, sometimes less elegant and comfortable, which he must establish on his own—perhaps the only real home he has ever established entirely by himself.

"This past weekend I had the two boys and I paid for one of them to rent a movie which he took to his mother's home to watch with his girlfriend," said one divorced man with a touch of bitterness. "He didn't want to bring her to my apartment because he was embarrassed to have her see how I live. And I am supporting the residence that they and their mother are living in."

Men often feel angry and resentful because they are forced to be part-time parents and to make sacrifices in their own lifestyle to support their former wives. In this chapter, we examine these as well as some of the other emotions that men experience—loneliness, sadness, fear and anxiety—and talk about how to deal with these feelings most effectively. Some men, for example, allow themselves to be consumed by their anger and let the fighting with their former wives go on far too long. We've talked with many of these individuals and what most of them need most desperately is to work through their anger to begin the process of planning for the future.

Anger is most hurtful to the people who are most important in your life: your children. It prevents you from focusing on their needs and safeguarding the relationship that you have with them. Since this is the focus of our entire book, we devote the first part of the chapter to answering some key questions involving your kids and their reactions to the divorce. Setting the right tone—dealing responsibly with your children's concerns and problems—is extremely important in the early stages of the divorce if you want to place your relationship with them on a firm foundation.

We assume that this is your primary concern.

1. WHEN SHOULD YOU TELL THE CHILDREN?

Certainly, the conventional advice from psychologists is not to tell the children until you're absolutely sure that you and your wife are going to get a divorce. (After all, you don't want to upset your children needlessly.) And then you should only tell them the nuts and bolts—the logistics of how things are going to work out, and not all the details of why the divorce is occurring.

But in the heat of the moment—with all the anger, the fears and anxieties—you often don't behave the way you'd like to believe you would. In my own case, my wife and I were fighting for three or four years before we got divorced.* And during that time the word "divorce" came up far too often and the kids understood what it meant, particularly my older child who was nine at the time. (My daughter was only four.) It had a traumatic effect on him. You could see on his face a feeling of helplessness—that his whole world would no longer be the same.

Another man explained that he and his wife never really used the word divorce. "But when kids see the fighting," he added, "and the name calling and the number of times you yell back 'I hate you', they know. Kids are smart and they talk to their

*All references to "I" in anecdotes or examples in the book refer to Bob Bernstein.

friends and they know what to expect."

We think you should make every effort to keep from discussing divorce in front of the children. But it often seems impossible, because most people don't have the capacity to be mature enough. Throwing out the word divorce in the midst of arguments is far more common than anyone is willing to admit. It's part of the fighting process, to threaten your spouse with divorce, when things break down and your fighting becomes irrational.

Unfortunately you and your wife may be out to harm one another verbally. Divorcing is a very "immaturing" process, both parties drop down the scale of maturity—as the reality hits, as the finances are being discussed, as the logistics of who is going to live where and how you're going to visit your children are worked out. All of those things are so painful that it's very easy to lose your ability to stay in control. People panic and throw out the wrong words. Going through a divorce is like going through adolescence—a time of irrational behavior.

Even if you don't use the word divorce, kids sense what's going on (as the man interviewed earlier in this section explained.) They know you, they can read your body language. They sense the tension, they hear the arguing, they are aware of the distance between you and your spouse. But love is not all or nothing. You can make many mistakes and still come out fine.

Children may experience the fighting and hear the word *divorce*; but as long as you assure them that you are not going to abandon them, and your actions reflect it, then you can short-circuit their fears. However, you must constantly repeat to your children that you still intend to see them on a regular basis. Too often this message is not delivered.

The critical thing is to establish right from the start that you're always going to be there, that you won't abandon them. Otherwise you'll have to overcome this impression later, and it will be far more difficult. Establish a positive pattern at the beginning. Then there's a much better chance that when you come to pick up your children during your visitation, they'll really want to be with you.

2. WHAT SHOULD YOU TELL THE CHILDREN?

Men have often explained to me that they wished they had said something to their children before leaving...they wished they had explained to them that a separation or divorce process was beginning. But then they admit to me that they wouldn't have known what to say.

The best thing many men can do is to talk to their children alone during visitation. First, a man might apologize to his children. For whether you feel you are right or wrong, you are fifty percent of the reason your children are being forced to deal with the divorce. So you have to be apologetic, but at the same time give them some reasonable explanation of why you will be better off and they will be better off in the future.

You might start out by saying, "I realize how badly you must be feeling because I'm feeling terrible, too." Then you might let silence intervene, and wait for the children to respond and talk about their own feelings. You should be willing to take your share of the blame. Don't make excuses or blame your wife for all the things that you feel she's done wrong. At this point, the children need to vent. So whatever they say to you, you just have to be prepared to take it. And if you take it, the problem will tend to dissipate much quicker..much quicker than if you try to make up all kinds of reasons to explain why the divorce is not your fault.

The child may need to vent more than once, for children need to revisit what is going on and express their feelings again and again. This is not an easy process, for them or for you. But it's something a man can do, especially if he is alone with his children and his spouse is not there. Your children need an atmosphere in which they can express their feelings. They need to feel secure in the fact that sometimes they can yell and scream at you and you will still love them.

As a father you are starting out with a large reservoir of good will from your children. You can build on that as long as you begin the process early after the separation—reassuring your children, letting them vent their feelings, and strengthening your relationship with them. Let them know the basics—where they'll be living, the visitation schedule, etc.—and that's all. Children may also be willing to help you with the process of building a new life—pitching in to advise you on decorating your new apartment, for example, planning meals and solidifying the bonds that tie you together.

> **Your children need an atmosphere in which they can express their feelings.**

3. WHAT REACTIONS SHOULD YOU EXPECT FROM YOUR KIDS?

Of course, these reactions will vary with the ages of the children.

Pre-school

Pre-school children respond best to structure, to getting up every day and anticipating routines— having their meals at the same time, seeing the same people. Divorce disrupts this routine, and very young children may react by reverting to earlier stages of development. Seeing one parent depart and fearing that the other parent may also leave, they may become very clingy and not want to be left alone. Sometimes pre-schoolers also act out and complain of physical ailments. They need to know that Dad is going to be visiting on certain days or weekends—they require that sense of stability and that routine. While routine is important for children of all ages, it is especially critical for these youngsters.

Elementary

My son was nine at the time of my divorce, and he really couldn't deal with it. He would have tantrums and create chaos. Once I began seeing him on a regular visitation schedule, we talked about his feelings regarding the divorce. He blamed both my wife and me for it. And I apologized to him and said that I hoped he could forgive me for whatever I had done. I also reassured my son that I would never leave and would continue to see him as often as I could. His deepest hope, of course, was that his mother and I would eventually get back together again. This hope remained alive even after she had married someone else.

Eventually, he stopped talking about the divorce, but I would bring it up again when I noticed that he was behaving out of character. I would ask my son what was bothering him, and often he would admit that it was something related to the divorce. For example, there were certain nights that he wanted to see me but couldn't because of the visitation schedule. At other times, when he was with me, he really preferred to be with his friends. That's frequently the problem with a visitation schedule—it's never very convenient for anyone. My son probably blamed me for putting him through this inconvenience, and he was nostalgic for the days when all of us lived together.

Teenagers

Contrary to what they say, teenagers need parents more than perhaps any other group. Parents are role models, they provide a mooring and a safe harbor during the turbulence of adolescence. When parents divorce, teenagers may become disillusioned and feel betrayed.

Dr. Judith Wallerstein, in her books *Surviving The Breakup* and *Second Chances,* writes about the results of her in-depth studies into the long-term impact of divorce on parents and children. When boys lose a meaningful relationship with their father, which often happens following a divorce, they can suffer a loss of self-confidence and self-esteem. This may result in lower achievement in school, less ambition and very limited goals for the future.

Girls often experience some of the same responses as boys. They may feel rejected by fathers who have left the home and then fail to visit them, as far too many fathers do. In addition, girls may be reluctant to develop close male/female relationships, fearful that they will end the same way as their parents' marriage. For many years afterward, they continue to harbor angry feelings toward their parents for not preventing the divorce and preserving the family in tact.

School often becomes the focal point for rebellion and irresponsibility among girls as well as boys. And it may be difficult to determine how much of this behavior is due to normal adolescence and how much results from the impact of the divorce. Teenagers can become very adept at blaming divorced parents for their problems in school and may try to make you feel very guilty. Under these circumstances, it is extremely important for you to communicate effectively with your former wife and establish consistent rules and expectations in dealing with your teenage son or daughter. If a teenager believes that one parent will accept lower standards of performance than the other, he may try to use this to his advantage.

At all stages of growth, a child's healthy development is dependent on the quality of the relationship provided by the custodial parent (usually the mother) as well as the visiting parent (usually the father).

> **School often becomes the focal point for rebellion and irresponsibility among girls as well as boys.**

4. HOW SHOULD YOU DEAL WITH A CHILD'S FEELINGS OF INSECURITY?

If there is any strange behavior coming from your children, more than likely it is due to the divorce and the changes in their lives. You should be sensitive to this problem and allow them to talk about it.

My son often manifested his insecurity by complaining about school. He criticized his teachers and fought against doing his homework. Perhaps he wasn't comfortable doing his homework in my new home or, when he visited me, he may have felt that this was only an occasion for fun and nothing else. Following a divorce, your child may change his perception of you from a parent to a "Santa Claus" figure—someone with whom he is only supposed to enjoy a good time.

The child's new perception may put you in a difficult position. You don't want to play the heavy and have a fight with your child, especially during a visitation when there is so little time for you to spend together. Nevertheless, you must also enforce some rules when your child is staying with you. It's important to know when to let children do what they want and when to dig in your heels and insist on some changes in their behavior.

My son and I had a number of conflicts over his homework, and often I had to force him to do it. This was especially true during the week when I had him for a sleep-over. Perhaps it was because we had so few hours together and he wanted to spend it together instead of working on his school lessons. It was a painful process, and I'm sure I made some mistakes in handling it. But, in the end, my son usually completed his homework satisfactorily.

5. WHAT SHOULD YOU DO IF YOUR CHILD BLAMES YOU FOR THE DIVORCE?

It's perfectly normal for the child to blame you. And this is a healthy reaction, within reason, of course. You should not let the child heap all of the blame on you. Too much is not fair and you have to say to the child: "There are some things that you don't understand and you have to trust me on this issue." A child who has a close relationship with you will accept this explanation, at least to some degree.

If the blame becomes out of proportion, you may need to talk to your former spouse and find out what she is telling the children. Or you may need to consider therapy for them. But remember that placing blame may be the child's way of trying to make some sense of the divorce. And it's how you handle this situation that makes the difference in the future of your relationship with your children.

It's most important not to blame your former wife in front of the child. If you start saying to your son or daughter: "Is your mother putting these ideas into your head?", it short-circuits any sharing that the child will do with you. Your child has an allegiance to both parents, and if you begin heaping blame on your ex-wife, the child will become very protective of her or simply stop talking. Instead of blaming your ex-wife, even if you sense that she is responsible, you're much better off to confront her directly.

6. WHEN IS THERAPY NECESSARY FOR A CHILD?

If the divorce is fairly difficult, you may need to consider therapy for a child. And you should try to get your former wife to agree with this decision and then share in the cost of it. For a child to have a third party with whom he can feel safe to express his feelings and who will help him get through that difficult early period after the divorce may be very, very important.

A therapist may be necessary if a child is exhibiting tremendous changes in behavior—acting out, or becoming very quiet, having nightmares, or suddenly doing poorly in school. These may be the warning signs. But to detect the signs you must maintain a close relationship with a child, and this requires a visitation schedule of more than every other weekend.

7. SHOULD YOU SHARE YOUR OWN FEELINGS WITH YOUR CHILDREN?

You certainly shouldn't talk about the anger you feel toward your ex-wife or all the pain and suffering you are experiencing from the divorce. These feelings may seem overwhelming, especially to small children. Instead, you should seek help with those emotions from a counselor or from your friends.

On the other hand, you should behave naturally. There

will be times when you can't control your sadness, and your children will notice it. If they ask whether you are sad, you should be honest and admit your feelings. You don't have to be specific; you might say: "I'm feeling sad about the divorce which is very hard and has brought about a lot of difficult changes in my life. But I'm working my way through it, as you are." That's a level of honesty that you need to have with your children if you want to maintain a meaningful relationship with them.

It may be difficult to keep from blaming the other parent and you may go too far at times. If this happens, apologize to your children and tell them that you went overboard in what you said about their mother. Explain that you were very upset, ask for their understanding and tell them that you will try to avoid a repeat of this incident in the future. Children are very receptive to an apology, especially if they know that you really mean it.

Some men have talked about cursing their ex-wives in front of their children and then regretting it afterward. Often the regrets don't begin until after a man's visitation is over and he realizes he has left his children with a heavy burden. Then he has to live with it until he sees them again—he can't even apologize until that time—and he hopes his children will even want to be with him so he can have the opportunity to apologize. Therefore, it's important to be very careful when you're talking about your ex-wife in front of your children.

> It is very important to be careful when you're talking about your ex-wife in front of your children.

8. WHAT FEELINGS WILL YOU BE EXPERIENCING ABOUT THE DIVORCE?

The full gamut. One especially angry man said: "I wanted to kill my wife. I felt defeat and outrage and betrayal."

Many men experience depression over the loss of a dream that they and their wives may have shared at one time—the dream of a home and a family and a life together. We don't think you're ever prepared for that dream to end and to confront the reality of starting all over again, especially if you're the person who leaves the house. Your physical world is really gone. I found myself leaving the house on a bitter, rainy night and looking for a motel. Sleeping in that motel was just agonizing.

As one man explained upon leaving his house: "I felt empty—my kids weren't going to be there when I woke up in the morning. I wasn't going to be able to get them ready for bed or read them bedtime stories."

A large part of your life is coming to a conclusion, and not a peaceful conclusion so you can put it on the shelf and remember it positively. It's a disaster of epic proportions and you tend to focus on your own predicament, very selfishly. In court, people always say you should worry about your children and how to take care of them. But the fact is, whether you want to admit it or not, you often think about yourself, first: "What's going to happen to me? Will I be able to find a place to live? Will I be able to afford a mortgage or a rent?"

Of course, if you can't carve out something for yourself, and take care of yourself, then the rest won't fall into place and you won't be able to care for your children. But that may just be a rationalization. No matter, it's natural to put yourself ahead of everyone else.

Anger is the most common emotion experienced by divorced men. Most of the men who call me on the telephone are very angry over something—a visitation schedule, for example, that seems unfair to them, or the fact that their ex-wife isn't abiding by that schedule and may be preventing them from seeing their children. Some men are also angry at their former spouse because she is involved with someone else.

On the other hand, many men talk about the feelings of relief they experience because they can finally put an end to an unhappy marriage. With the relief may also come feelings of anxiety: How will I deal with the loneliness of being single? Can I create a new home for myself? Can I afford to pay child support for my children and perhaps alimony to my former wife? How good a father can I be in my new role as the non-custodial parent?

9. HOW DO YOU COPE WITH THESE FEELINGS?

Men may have made considerable strides in expressing their feelings over the past twenty years, but there is no doubt that they still have a long way to go. Most of our brethren have no trouble expressing anger—this is one emotion that seems quite acceptable. But too many men seem to get stuck in their anger and years later they're still there—railing at their lawyers for not properly representing them, at the court system for imposing an unfair divorce settlement upon them, at their ex-wives for preventing them from seeing their children. While all of these complaints may contain an element of truth, it does no good for men to become obsessed with them.

Men need a forum in which to express their anger, and move on to more productive pursuits. Otherwise this anger can poison their efforts to negotiate successfully with their ex-wives or maintain a satisfying relationship with their children. Often the best forum is a men's support group. In Connecticut, for example, there are local chapters of the Divorced Men's Association as well as support groups run by Big Brothers/Big Sisters. And similar organizations exist in many other parts of the country. A therapist may also prove extremely helpful, or an understanding friend.

In addition to their anger, men also need the opportunity to express the other emotions often associated with divorce—loneliness, sadness, anxiety, fear, etc. These are generally much harder for men to acknowledge or to discuss openly because they have very little practice at it. But if you can't experience these feelings, it is often very difficult to understand and empathize with the feelings of others—whether it's a woman or your own kids.

10. WHAT KIND OF PLANNING NEEDS TO BE DONE EARLY IN THE DIVORCE PROCESS?

Most men are concerned about money and how their lives are going to be limited by what their new expenses will be. They're anxious over finding a new place to live and beginning a new life in a way that's affordable, after paying alimony, etc. They may also feel angry over their predicament because somewhat irrationally men believe that their money should remain their money and not be shared with a former spouse.

Instead of focusing on this problem, men must begin to look at the bigger picture and plan for the long term future. They must ask: "How can I come out of this divorce being fair to my former wife and at the same time being a good parent?" They must look five or six years down the line, decide what they want, and how to get there with the existing resources, and they must start this planning early in the divorce process.

If you want to be an actively involved parent, for example, you can't take a new job that's three states away. You must work and live in a place that's near your children—in a home that's comfortable for them and in a neighborhood that's safe. You must also try to get along with your ex-wife—that's if you want to see your children with as little friction as possible. Treat your ex-wife as you would a business client so you can reap the benefits of quality time with your kids.

All of these considerations will lead you inevitably to the conclusion that you have to pay child support and perhaps alimony, whether you like it or not, because it's the only way you'll have a chance of being with your children. And if you're going to pay this money, then you have to look at the other parts of your life (your vacations, for example) and determine where you can cut back to afford the payments. You may want to delay this planning process and continue to fight with your ex-wife because it's much easier. But the casualties will only be your children and your relationship with them.

11. HOW HONEST SHOULD YOU BE WITH YOUR WIFE?

You should rely on the advice of your attorney. But remember that in terms of finances and assets, there's nothing you can hide. Each side can find out what the other side has. Further, if you are ever caught hiding anything and it is discovered, this will work to your disadvantage in the divorce settlement.

12. HOW DO YOU DEAL WITH FRIENDS DURING THE DIVORCE?

This can be very difficult. As a result of a divorce, you may lose the friendship of married couples who were friendly with you and your wife. Couples tend to befriend other couples, and this bond is broken as a result of divorce. However, friendships with individuals may continue.

In addition, since the patterns of your life are now changing, you will probably seek out and develop new friendships. These relationships provide an important support system during the divorce and afterward. Friends can give you a place to spend time, for the breakup of a marriage often provides you with additional time on your hands that was previously consumed by the routine responsibilities of family life. Friends can help you get through those awkward, lonely hours with dinner invitations, for instance. Your friends can also provide you with the opportunity to vent your feelings—feelings that are much better expressed to them than to your children.

13. HOW DO YOU DEAL WITH PARENTS AND OTHER RELATIVES DURING THE DIVORCE?

Your parents usually want to be involved with your children and you should encourage them to maintain the same relationship that existed prior to the divorce. Grandparents have a valuable perspective that no one else can offer your children. And they provide the security of an extended family that may be critically important during the divorce.

Parents can also give you essential help in raising a child. For example, you may be called unexpectedly out of town on business during a visitation period and need someone to care for your children, or you may require assistance with shopping, cooking and other household chores. Grandparents can be your best resources in these situations.

Unfortunately, it is often difficult, if not impossible to retain a cordial relationship with your in-laws during a divorce. Under most circumstances their primary concern will be with supporting your former wife. And if her attitude toward you is especially rancorous, it is almost certain to affect your in-laws, as well. Most grandparents, however, want to stay involved with their grandchildren. If the divorce between you and your wife remains relatively amicable, you may still be able to retain a relationship with your in-laws, centered primarily on your children. Such a relationship only strengthens their extended family and may prove extremely beneficial.

14. WHO IS YOUR GREATEST ENEMY?

You may think it's your ex-wife. But for most men, it's themselves. The prejudice against men as parents, which results in women usually winning custody, or the prevailing attitude that divorced men are "deadbeat Dads" who don't pay child support is rooted in a great deal of data. Most men don't want to be single parents, although they also don't want to be denied access to their children. Nevertheless, 40 percent of all children rarely if ever see their fathers after a divorce, regardless of the visitation schedule.

And about 1/3 of all men refuse to pay child support. So a man who really wants to remain involved with his children and abide by his divorce agreement faces some significant barriers in the eyes of society.

None of these barriers, however, is too great to overcome. You can remain an active and involved parent during the divorce process and afterwards. But it takes the ability to cope effectively with your emotions, to negotiate successfully with your ex-wife, and above all, to often put your children first. In fact, it may not be much of an exaggeration to say that their needs must always be your highest priority.

> **Remember that the barriers you encounter are not too great to overcome.**

CHAPTER II

THE PSYCHOLOGICAL ISSUES OF DIVORCE

Divorce not only disrupts a marriage and a family, it profoundly shakes a man's entire life. Next to the death of a loved one, it may be the most stressful event that anyone can experience. Naturally, divorce stirs up a variety of conflicting feelings. Some men try to deny them and hope they will go away; instead, they frequently resurface and undermine a man's ability to develop an intimate relationship with another woman or maintain close relationships with his kids. A more constructive approach is to acknowledge these feelings and work through them, which will enable you to enjoy a far more satisfying life.

No matter how unsatisfying his marriage may have been, a man often finds himself wishing to return to his former wife and the old routines of his home. This is a typical reaction to change... a natural reluctance to let go of the past which defined

This chapter is written by David B. London, M.D. He has a private practice of adult, adolescent and family psychiatry and is Assistant Clinical Professor of Psychiatry at Yale University.

so much of who you were. And it may take a number of months before you have begun to adjust to a new lifestyle. This period of adjustment will seem like an emotional roller coaster—with euphoric highs and depressing lows. You can expect to experience a profound sadness as you mourn the loss of your former life and try to embark on a new one. Many men also regard divorce as a major failure, for which they blame themselves as well as their ex-wives. Unfortunately this may be expressed in self-destructive behavior such as alcoholism and drug abuse or in furious outbursts against a former spouse and even defenseless children.

Dealing effectively with the feelings that surround divorce is one of the major tasks that confronts every man during the post-divorce period. It has been said that time is the great healer, so the sadness, anger and pain will certainly begin to diminish as the months go by. But time is not enough, and a man must be prepared to undertake an active role in working through his feelings. If anger is a serious problem, professional help from a therapist may be necessary. Relaxation exercises, meditation and various other spiritual rituals may also assist you in dealing with the stress that leads to frustration and anger and the tendency to blame the divorce on others.

The upheaval of divorce offers you an opportunity to redefine your sense of self and re-evaluate what's really important to you. This can not only enable you to feel more comfortable with yourself but also to derive greater pleasure in your role as a father.

15. HOW DO YOU ACHIEVE EMOTIONAL SEPARATION FROM YOUR WIFE?

Divorce usually occurs after an extended period of conflict, frustration and stress. So we would expect that couples would have no trouble separating emotionally, by the time their legal divorce actually happens. For many couples, however, true separation is not possible because their continuing responsibilities as parents bring them in constant contact with each other. In addition, a husband and wife who have been married for a long period—whether happily or not—will probably retain an ongoing sense of attachment to each other in spite of the divorce. When your entire identity is defined by your marital status and family relationships, it is understandable that the loss of this role creates a gap in your life. Thus, it's natural to cling to this familiar role regardless of how unpleasant your marriage may have been.

As we mentioned in the previous chapter, a man often experiences an emptiness in the pit of his stomach when a marriage ends. Men generally see divorce as a failure, they feel frightened and needy, and have a longing to return to the marriage relationship, although they know rationally that it is over. In order to go back to the comfort of their homes, their kids, and their usual routines, men may begin to distort the history of their marriages and even try to persuade themselves that it wasn't so bad, after all.

A man's efforts to undo the divorce process and rebuild the marriage are a natural protest against emotional detachment. To detach means to let go. You must acknowledge the loss, feel the pain and sorrow, cry, get support, accept the fact that there were good and bad things about your marriage, and feel angry over the disappointment that your hopes for the marriage didn't materialize. You must also understand that the process of letting go will take time. At least six to nine months are required to mourn the loss of your marriage and get comfortable with it. Allow up to two years before you really feel free of the bond.

16. WHY IS STABILITY IN YOUR LIFESTYLE IMPORTANT DURING THE DIVORCE PERIOD?

Without question, everyone needs to bond with somebody else. The danger in the early stages of divorce is to rush into another relationship and try to satisfy your emotional needs for love, acceptance and belonging. This can only create confusion. It is far better to realize that it will take time to heal the scars from your marriage. And while this process is going on, the best possible relationship for you is one based on friendship and companionship where there is no pressure for love and long-term commitment.

This is a good chance to build new friendships or rekindle old ones that were not so central during your marital life. It's also an opportunity to invest energy into taking care of yourself—whether through physical fitness, relaxation, personal and spiritual development, vacationing, hobbies, or simply completing personal and professional projects that you have put on the back burner. Needless to say, it's also essential to build your relationships with your children.

Divorce is an extremely stressful event, and it's important to integrate the loss of your partner into your life. So minimize any additional stresses and try to avoid making any other major life changes. Don't jump into a new identity, a new career, an expensive endeavor, or embark on an extensive move or an intimate relationship. Wait until the dust settles so you can see clearly what you really want to do with your life.

There is a lot to be said for patiently waiting, at least during the first two years following a divorce, before beginning major life changes. You may be reminded of your recent past by staying with the relative sameness of your life. But you won't regret it in the long run. The quiet stability of your current life structure will enable you to absorb the loss of your wife, the end of your marriage, and the change in your family, and give you time to adjust to your new status.

17. HOW DO YOU COPE WITH THE SAD FEEL-INGS THAT OVERWHELM AND DEPRESS YOU?

Although all of us know that sadness is a natural feeling, there is a sense of discomfort when you feel sad. Somehow you imagine that you're not normal, less than what you should be, that you've been cheated or done something wrong. It may seem paradoxical, but if you can allow yourself to feel sad and weak when you're truly hurt, then you can be strong. But if you defend against sadness by pretending that everything is all right when it's not, of if you feel guilty over your sadness, then you're setting yourself up to get depressed.

Depression is not bad or abnormal. In fact, a certain amount of depression is a good thing, for it allows us to reflect on where we've been and what is truly important to us. Unfortunately, there may also be a tendency to distort what you see. When you're depressed, the world always appears worse than it is, and the danger of being depressed for too long is that you become confused and start to believe in all the dark images of yourself.

In divorce, it's easy to feel like a failure—whether the divorce was your idea or your ex-wife's. Divorce signifies that something didn't work out, and everyone can see it. You feel ashamed because you've received a blow to your male ego. Regardless of how old you are, how well-educated, how mature, or how many friends and nurturing family members you have, divorce is still a blow to your sense of self. Your identity is shaken and it's not uncommon to feel intensely disappointed in yourself. This may kindle a fury that leads to self-destructive behaviors such as alcohol and drug abuse, inappropriate interactions at work, with your children, or most commonly, with your ex-wife. A tendency to blame yourself for the divorce can alternate with blaming others for something that is not blameworthy.

When you find yourself being annoyed at petty things, consider that you are caught up in feeling disappointed in yourself. Allow yourself to feel the hurt, and don't blame your ex-wife for it. Take time to heal. Don't be hard on yourself. Instead try to change your perspective and look at things from another angle. Tell yourself a story that makes you sound good. Believe in yourself!

18. HOW DO YOU CONTROL YOUR ANGER?

When a man's frustration erupts into repeated angry outbursts that offend others or, even worse, result in violence, then it's necessary to examine that behavior carefully. More than likely, the stress of divorce is getting to you and you're reacting negatively to perceived hurts and injustices. It's all too easy to dump your feelings on your ex-wife, burden your children with your anger towards her, behave destructively toward your family, their property, their sense of security, or begin to abuse your own mind and body.

Why not seek a constructive outlet for your anger? In the previous chapter we talked about Divorced Men's Associations and other support groups as an excellent forum in which to vent your angry feelings. Physical exercise and competitive sports also provide a way to channel your anger productively.

If you know you have a problem with your anger and if it was a major source of stress in your marriage, then you may need to seek professional help. Psychotherapy with a licensed clinician—such as a psychiatrist, psychologist, psychiatric social worker or other professional—can provide a stable structure in which to contain your angry impulses. A clinician can also teach you coping mechanisms to transform destructive anger into productive energy. When you chose a therapist, try to select someone who makes you feel comfortable—someone with whom you can talk easily. Perhaps a good friend can give you a recommendation of someone who will be helpful.

Relaxation training is also useful to decrease stress. Your

are less likely to become angry if you are relaxed or know how to relax in the face of frustration. Yoga and meditation can bring you peace of mind, too.

19. HOW DO YOU WORK ON ACCEPTING THE CHANGE IN YOUR LIFE?

Adapting to changes like divorce is a stressful process that requires time. Without question, there are many losses, but with each one there is an opportunity for a new undertaking, a new commitment, a new start. But judicious timing is essential for making these changes if you want to avoid premature decisions. You don't want to contaminate a new part of your life with unresolved issues stemming from your marriage and divorce. By gradually letting go of the attachment to your ex-wife and your role as husband as well as working through your sorrow and anger, you will begin to feel a renewed sense of vitality. This is different from an anxious or compulsive pressure to immediately rush into an intimate relationship or make a major life change.

The craving to feel whole again with meaning in your life is very strong, but you must first focus on doing some inner psychological work. That's what *acceptance* means. It's a reorientation to a situation that once caused frustration and conflict; now you recognize that a change has occurred and you must adapt to survive. This reorientation often stirs up many psychological issues that go beyond the marriage and your relationship to your children. Your sense of identity is revisited with many searching questions: Who am I? What kind of man am I? How much time is left in my life? What can I do now that will compensate for my feelings of failure? What is my ability to have an intimate relationship? Do I ever want to marry again? What is the role of work in my life? What is really important to me?

In considering such questions, it is natural to feel worried and fearful in the wake of divorce, but there is no substitute for a disciplined review of all these issues until you feel settled about them. Make time in your routine to revisit these questions and revise your responses to them as time unfolds. When the answers seem consistent over a few months, you can feel somewhat assured that you have come to terms with them and you're ready to move on with your life.

20. HOW CAN YOU BEGIN TO DEVELOP MORE SATISFYING ADULT RELATIONSHIPS IN THE FUTURE?

A man unconsciously reacts to his wife as if she were his mother. He expects the same sort of responses from her—unconditional nurturing and acceptance as well as the gratification of all his needs. This can sorely interfere with a man's appreciation of who his wife is in her own right. In most cases divorce is a result not only of a man's inability to reconcile his past relationship with his mother so that it doesn't interfere with his marriage, but also his wife's inability to do the same thing. Much of the conflict for a couple in a troubled marriage revolves around not meeting each other's needs. Rather than blaming your ex-wife for this problem, recognize your responsibility for the divorce and redefine your own expectations from an intimate relationship.

This may involve re-evaluating your definition of masculinity. The older your are, the greater the chances that you were brought up with traditional models of maleness and femaleness. While these models have been challenged in recent years as a result of the woman's movement and other social forces, many men have refused to adjust their image of what it means to be a male. If your partner's expectations of a man conflict with the role that you think a man should play, it can create problems in any of your future relationships. You may need to decide if you want to make some changes in your definition of the masculine role, not only as it pertains to male-female relationships but also to the relationship with your children.

If you choose to change your notion of what it means to be a man, there is a wealth of support. The Men's Movement provides considerable opportunities, with popular books such as Robert Bly's *Iron John* and Sam Keen's *Fire In the Belly,* as well as all types of men's groups that will help you rethink who you are. Redefining yourself doesn't mean that you must become a spineless wimp but only a more complete man—one who combines strength and sensitivity.

In order to derive more satisfaction in your life and your relationships, it is essential to recapture your spiritual center. This may mean strengthening the ties to your religion or finding other spiritual activities that will fill you with light and healing energy. Performing simple rituals throughout the day takes very little time but can be very effective in centering yourself. These rituals include: taking a short walk, closing your eyes and imagining yourself in a pleasant place, drawing clockwise spirals with a pencil and imagining greater freedom with each turn of the spiral, preparing a special meal for yourself, contemplating nature, and, finally, prayer.

When you feel overwhelmed with hurt and sadness, picture your heart full of arrows; then take the arrows out, and massage your heart until it feels good. You can also get rid of negative emotion by visualizing it as an object, then wrapping it in a package and throwing it away. Don't underestimate the power of positive thinking and mental imagery; increasingly, scientific research is documenting the relationship between the content of your active mind and your physical health.

> **It is essential to recapture your spiritual center.**

CHAPTER III

DIVORCE AND THE LAW

One man told us that before his divorce he had never consulted an attorney, but since that time he never seemed to be without one. Since divorce is a legal process, you will probably discover that a great deal of your time is spent with your lawyer. And while some books recommend that you represent yourself, we strongly believe that issues such as custody, child support, and visitation are far too complicated to be handled without the help of a trained professional.

One of the most important questions confronting you in beginning the divorce process is how to find an attorney who seems to understand your needs as a divorcing father and who will help you achieve the results you want in your divorce action. This does not mean a "cutthroat" lawyer who will try to exact a pound of flesh from your wife. These people usually succeed in destroying any relationship that still remains for both of you, which makes communication after the divorce almost impossible and dooms to failure any attempts at jointly raising your children, no matter how well-intended.

The success of your case, however, will not depend entirely on your attorney. You must also expect to play a key role in a number of critical areas: 1. providing your lawyer with accurate information regarding your finances and the history of your marriage (see Appendix B); 2. carefully thinking through your position regarding issues such as spousal support (alimony), visitation, child support and the division of property; 3. preparing yourself to participate in the different stages of the divorce process; 4. always recognizing what level of service you can legitimately anticipate from your attorney and when you may be demanding too much. Of course, if your lawyer fails to meet acceptable standards, don't hesitate to hire a new one.

Although divorce cases have been traditionally settled by our adversarial legal process, many experts now believe that there may be a better approach—one that enables divorcing couples to work together and create a sound basis on which to place their relationship following the divorce. This alternative is called mediation. In this chapter, we look at the mediation process and compare the costs to hiring attorneys. As one divorce lawyer, who is also a mediator, put it: Fully 70 percent of all divorce cases can be settled by mediation. Perhaps this is an option for you to seriously consider.

21. HOW DO YOU FIND THE "RIGHT" ATTORNEY?

Many men feel scared and vulnerable when their divorce begins. One divorced Dad told us he wanted to hand over all of his problems to someone who would immediately take care of them so he wouldn't need to worry any longer. His first thought was to work with a person he knew, so he called a friend who was a lawyer and asked her to represent him. Unfortunately, her specialty was not matrimonial law, and it soon became clear that she was unfamiliar with many of the finer legal points relating to his case. Several weeks later he was forced to replace her, which was a very painful experience.

When the divorce crisis starts to break over your head, the natural inclination is to hire a lawyer quickly so you'll have someone to represent your interests. Resist the temptation, because if you retain the wrong attorney it can cost you valuable time and negotiating points. While you may not want to be methodical in the midst of a crisis, it is the best way to find the right attorney.

Talk to friends, family members and business colleagues who have gone through a divorce and ask them for recommendations. Contact your local bar association, which will suggest several attorneys in the area who specialize in divorce. You might also call any attorneys whom you know and find out if they can recommend any of their colleagues in the field of matrimonial law.

The next step is to interview several of these lawyers and evaluate their expertise. Don't be afraid to call and make appointments. Most lawyers will give you a free hour of consultation, which is plenty of time to ask questions, find out how they will handle your case, and determine if you want any of these individuals to represent you.

> **Take time to find the right attorney.**

22. WHAT QUESTIONS SHOULD YOU ASK TO EVALUATE AN ATTORNEY?

Whether you decide to interview lawyers by telephone or in person, there are several key questions that you should always ask them.

1. How much matrimonial work do you handle? We think you should only work with an attorney whose specialty is family law. State legislatures are continually passing new statutes affecting areas such as custody, child support, visitation and property settlements. If your attorney is not aware of what the legal system requires, he is not going to be fully prepared to represent you successfully.

2. What results have you achieved in cases that go to trial? Although most cases are negotiated between the attorneys and never reach trial, some do. If you feel that there are enough issues of conflict between you and your spouse so that a trial may be necessary, you must be assured that your lawyer is not only prepared to go to trial but stands an excellent chance of achieving success.

3. How many child custody cases have you handled, especially for men? You must be sure that your lawyer is sensitive to your needs as a father and your desire to spend as much time as possible with your children. She should be able to realistically appraise your chances of achieving sole custody, if

you want it, fully comprehend the advantages and disadvantages of joint custody (we'll talk more about different types of custody in another part of this chapter) as well as what type of visitation schedule you can expect to receive. You might also ask her to briefly tell you what results she has achieved for other men.

4. What will be the strategy for my case? Quickly outline your situation and expectations to each attorney and ask them how they might proceed to handle your case. This information will enable you to evaluate them as professionals, compare their approaches and decide whom to hire.

5. Will you be the only one handling my case? Frequently an experienced lawyer works with an assistant, known as an associate, who handles many of the details in each case. Find out who the associates might be and when you can meet them. It's important to evaluate them as well. However, you should always make sure that the attorney you hire will be the one actually appearing in court for you. Each attorney juggles many cases simultaneously, and you must decide if he has enough time to represent you effectively.

23. WHAT SHOULD YOU EXPECT TO PAY FOR A DIVORCE?

Rates will vary, so be sure to ask the attorneys for their rates when you interview them. Lawyers frequently bill by the hour, or part of an hour, and the meter starts running whether they're talking to you on the telephone, asking you questions in their office, preparing a legal document in your case, or representing you in court (sometimes the rate is higher for time spent in court). If a lawyer agrees to handle your divorce, he may ask for a retainer—a fee paid at the beginning which is applied to the total cost of his work on the case. These retainers will vary, too. Once the retainer is used up, then the billing begins, and you should ask how often you can expect to be billed. Many men may need to negotiate a long-term payment plan, if they don't have the funds to pay their attorney immediately. Find out if your lawyer will accept this method of payment.

24. WHAT INFORMATION WILL YOUR LAWYER NEED FROM YOU?

Lawyers interviewed for this book mentioned that during their initial consultations they commonly asked clients for financial information. This includes their assets and liabilities as well as their income and expenses—information that is vitally important in determining possible spousal support (alimony) as well as child support. You will be asked to include regular expenses, such as mortgage payments and taxes, income from your job or other sources—stocks and bonds, for example—as well as the value of assets like your house, your mutual funds, or retirement plans and any debts you may currently owe. Your attorney may also ask for supporting information such as tax returns, 1099 forms or W2s.

Try to be as honest and accurate as possible, for as one

lawyer writes: "Rest assured that if you forget to include an asset or income, your spouse's lawyer will contend that you did not forget, you lied." And if you have to go to court, any negative impression that you make on the judge can have an enormous impact on the final outcome of your case.

In addition to the financial information, lawyers also ask for a marital history. While this may be somewhat painful to write, you should try to be as complete as possible. Begin chronologically with the date of your marriage and include all relevant information, such as any jobs that you and your spouse have filled, current employability, levels of educational achievement, reasons for the breakdown of the marriage, efforts to improve the relationship, names and ages of your children, any special problems they may have, as well as the roles and responsibilities of you and your spouse in raising them. This information guides your lawyer in his efforts to negotiate a fair agreement, while also saving time (and money) that he would otherwise have to spend talking to you(see Appendix B).

25. WHAT IS DISCOVERY?

Some men try to hide financial assets or understate their net worth to reduce the size of their alimony and support payments. However, your spouse's lawyer can simply request this information through a process known as *discovery*. This means that the court simply grants attorneys the power to subpoena documents or submit written questions that you must answer under oath.

Information is often obtained through a deposition, in which anyone who has knowledge of your marriage is required to give oral testimony under oath. Your lawyer may take your wife's deposition and her lawyer will question you in a deposition. All the testimony is transcribed by a court reporter, who is present during the questioning, which generally takes place in lawyers' offices. Thorough preparation for your deposition with your attorney is crucial, as an unprepared deponent can severely damage a case.

26. WHY ARE YOUR EXPECTATIONS OF YOUR ATTORNEY IMPORTANT?

In business there is a process called "Total Quality Management" which is based on the premise that your customers always come first, and you should strive to satisfy their expectations. In your relationship with an attorney, you are the customer. So he needs to know your expectations—what results you hope to achieve in the divorce action. And any competent attorney will tell you if your expectations are realistic.

On every issue, you should have an ideal that you want, a minimum that you can live with, as well as a middle position that is still acceptable. Unfortunately, when it comes to child support, many men feel that all three positions are the same—the lowest figure possible. That's usually not realistic, nor is it fair to your children. You need to think rationally about these issues and separate your feelings for your wife from what is fair in each situation.

You also need to do some preparation before seeing your attorney. Know what your house is worth, for example, what you think would be a fair amount to receive, as well as the maximum you want and the minimum you will accept. Follow the same decision-making process for alimony and visitation. Remember, when you consult an attorney, time is money. So the more preparation you can do, the less time you have to spend in a lawyer's office discussing problems or even arguing over what seems equitable.

If you have trouble thinking through some of these issues alone, talk to a friend or find a support group. Other men who have been through the same experience may prove extremely helpful in broadening your perspective.

27. HOW CAN YOU WORK WITH YOUR LAWYER MOST EFFECTIVELY?

To reiterate—be prepared, whether you're at a meeting in your lawyer's office or calling on the telephone with a question. And don't become frustrated if your attorney isn't immediately available to take your call. Lawyers handle a large number of cases simultaneously and they may be talking to another client when you telephone them. In fact, it may even take two or three days before your attorney can return your call. We, therefore, suggest that you don't contact your attorney with every question that enters your mind. Write down your questions as you think of them and at the end of the week call with your entire list. This shows your attorney that you are well-organized, and it's far more likely to elicit a prompt response. If you are constantly calling with one question at a time, you lawyer is not as likely to accord you the same prompt consideration.

Also keep in mind that your lawyer is only there to handle your legal questions, and nothing more. Many men want their lawyer to be their therapist or confessor and become upset when he doesn't seem to have time or training to function in these roles.

In some cases, you may need to act as your own attorney, which is often far more productive than simply sitting around and criticizing your lawyer for being too busy to represent you adequately. If you are prepared, there are critical moments when you'll be able to make good suggestions that may prove extremely beneficial to your attorney.

Here's an example. I went back to court three or four years after my divorce to change the visitation schedule with my daughter, whom I had with me every other weekend and for a dinner and sleep-over during the week. The lawyer who usually represented me was not available that day so he sent his associate to court. He explained to the judge that I wanted to extend my daughter's weekend visit until Monday morning; my former wife, however, wanted her back on Sunday night. After listening to both sides of the argument, the judge finally said that his only interest was in keeping the number of hours that my daughter spent with me and her mother unchanged. At that point, I should have told my lawyer that I would give up the sleep-over during the week (and take my daughter home after dinner) so I could keep her overnight on Sunday. This is what my daughter wanted, too. But I wasn't prepared and missed the opportunity.

My lawyer didn't think of this compromise, either. So the visitation schedule remained the same, although I had spent a significant amount of money on legal fees.

28. WHEN SHOULD YOU CHANGE LAWYERS?

Some men become so frustrated that they decide to change attorneys. While this action may be justified—especially in cases where your attorney has proven over and over again very unresponsive to your questions—it is best to make an appointment to see your lawyer before making a change. As one lawyer put it: "I've had a lot of new clients come to me simply because of a communications breakdown with their previous attorney, who was really doing a good job in handling their case. Lawyers do get busy and sometimes a client has to be persistent."

Some lawyers, however, simply don't represent their clients effectively. If a lawyer keeps promising results that never materialize, that's a sign that something is wrong. One attorney we interviewed described another member of the bar who promised every man that he would get sole custody for him. After spending all of the man's money, he still only received joint custody and the custodial parent was his wife.

An attorney may also just agree to do whatever you want instead of realistically appraising your chances of getting the desired outcome. This type of representation will only bring you serious disappointments.

29. SHOULD YOU HIRE A "CUTTHROAT" LAWYER?

No matter how tempting, generally, the answer is no. A lawyer whose reputation is to "go for the jugular" is not serving your best interests, and, as a consequence, may impair the relationship with your children following the divorce. Overly aggressive tactics simply increase the hurt and anger experienced by you and your wife. It's like a cold war in which each side continuously raises the threat of destruction, and almost any meaningful dialogue becomes impossible. Whether you like it or not, you will need to continue communicating with your former spouse following the divorce because both of you play a critical role in raising your children.

30. HOW LONG SHOULD THE DIVORCE PROCESS LAST?

It depends on the severity of the conflict between you and your spouse. In Connecticut, for example, the dissolution of a marriage process begins when one party issues a Complaint to the other. The person who begins the action is the plaintiff; the defendant is the one who receives the Complaint, which is served by a sheriff.

The Complaint directs the defendant to obtain an attorney within a specified number of days and file papers with the court. Information contained in most Complaints includes: when and where you were married, the fact that at least one spouse has fulfilled the state's residency requirement for divorce, as well as the names and birth dates of any minor children. The Complaint also describes the reason for the divorce— usually irretrievable breakdown of the marriage (known as "no-fault"). In addition, the Complaint mentions issues such as alimony, child support, custody, and property division. Try not to be intimidated by a Complaint, which generally asks for everything, including the "kitchen sink". The Complaint is often generated by the attorney's word processor, and tends to include a myriad of requests, some of which may not ultimately be sought against you.

At this time the lawyers for each spouse will try to agree on temporary amounts to be paid for alimony and child support as well as temporary custody and visitation schedules. Some lawyers caution that you should be wary when agreeing to temporary custody and visitation arrangements. These have a way of becoming permanent in the final divorce settlement, because the judge will not want to upset your child's routine.

If there is no agreement on any of these issues, the attorneys will need to file motions or go to court for temporary orders. These procedures take time and extend the length of the divorce process; they can also be expensive. If there are disagreements over custody, the court may require an investigation of you, your spouse and your children to determine which arrangement serves the best interests of everyone, especially the children. This process may be slow to get started since many cases are usually under investigation. While a smooth, conflict-free divorce may be completed in several months, a rancorous case can drag on for several years. Most cases eventually reach agreement at some point, and after a final brief hearing in court the judge will dissolve your marriage.

31. WHAT IS "FAIR" IN TERMS OF SPOUSAL SUPPORT AND CHILD SUPPORT?

In the past many wives received spousal support, also called alimony, because they had spent most of their adult lives as parents/homemakers, with little prospect of supporting themselves. Today, since women work and many continue to hold jobs while raising families, alimony is awarded to fewer women and the duration is usually limited. The amount of alimony is dependent on a variety of factors, including the length of the marriage, the amount of your income, your wife's income and her ability to earn a living, the number of children you have and their ages, and the assets your wife receives as part of the settlement. Alimony can terminate on your ex-wife's death, remarriage or cohabitation.

One way to reduce the amount of alimony you must pay, is to minimize your former wife's need for it—help her obtain a job, if she isn't working; pay for her to receive additional education so she is more employable; or pay off any of her debts.

The amount of child support, which is determined by guidelines established in most states, is based on a percentage of your income as the non-custodial parent or the incomes of you and your spouse. Generally, you must continue to make support payments until a child reaches majority or graduates from high school, whichever comes first.

Unless it is written into the divorce agreement, neither parent is obliged to pay for their child's college education. As a result, many children who plan to attend college suddenly find that no one is willing to help them with tuition costs. And, once again, they are victimized by the divorce process. Therefore, we strongly recommend that you and your former spouse make some provision for a child's post-secondary education, put the agreement in writing and have it recognized by the court. The current tuition costs at Ivy League colleges are beyond the financial means of most of us. Instead, use your State University tuition, room and board as a guideline, or a cap, for the amount of money you and your former wife are prepared to pay toward your children's education. Leaving them without any financial support is simply unfair and not in their best interests.

32. WHAT HAPPENS IF YOU DON'T PAY YOUR SUPPORT PAYMENTS?

In 1984, Congress passed legislation requiring state and local governments to help custodial parents collect child support. If you don't make support payments, the court can send an Order of Withholding to your employer requiring that these payments be garnished from your paycheck. However, this approach will not be very effective if a man is self-employed. In such a case, a man who is delinquent in his support payments may be issued a contempt citation, required to appear at a hearing and forced to make a lump sum payment.

In addition, the state and Federal government can seize

your income tax return and apply this money to delinquent support. Some men who have been especially negligent in making regular payments have appeared in wanted posters for Deadbeat Dads, and still others have even found themselves serving time in jail.

Even with all these measures at the disposal of the law enforcement authorities, only a small percentage of Deadbeat Dads are ever forced to pay up. It can be especially difficult to find men who have left the state where their families reside and force them to abide by their divorce agreements. This is a significant reason why responsible Dads have such a hard time in convincing the judicial system to respect their parental requests.

33. SHOULD YOU TRY TO SETTLE YOUR DIVORCE WITHOUT GOING TO TRIAL?

Very few divorce cases ever reach trial. One reason is that most divorcing spouses succeed in coming to some kind of agreement beforehand. A trial is very costly in lawyer's fees, with little or no guarantee that the judge's ruling will be in your favor. There are numerous stories of cases that seemed headed for trial only to be settled by the opposing attorneys on the courthouse steps or in the corridor leading to the courtroom. Although attorneys may say that you are entitled to your day in court, they generally prefer to avoid a trial because the outcome is often uncertain.

34. IS OUR ADVERSARIAL LEGAL SYSTEM THE BEST WAY TO DEAL WITH DIVORCE CASES?

One lawyer, who is also a mediator, says that fully 70 percent of all divorce cases should be handled by mediation instead of litigation. The adversarial legal system often just exacerbates the tension and deepens the bad feelings that exist between you and your spouse. As you and your attorneys do battle over issues from child support to property settlements, painful wounds are inflicted that are slow to heal. The resulting scars can prevent the type of cooperation that is necessary to raise healthy, well-adjusted children. In short, everybody loses.

35. WHAT IS MEDIATION?

Mediation is an alternative to the usual divorce process. It occurs when a neutral party—such as a therapist, an attorney, or a team of both people—sits down with a husband and wife to enable them to reach a divorce agreement.

Couples who engage in mediation recognize that this is not an adversarial process. It is based on negotiation and cooperation and the ability to put yourself in the shoes of the other person. People considering mediation have often attended therapy together so they have begun the process of trying to negotiate their differences. As one mediator put it: "A vengeful attitude is not appropriate." Individuals in mediation must be able to separate their own conflicts from the interests of their children. So you must think carefully about these issues before sitting down with a mediator.

In contrast to lawyers, "we don't represent the two people, we represent the process to the agreement," a mediator explained. "We try to keep ourselves focused on what we're doing here, and help them through this process."

36. WHEN SHOULD YOU CONSIDER MEDIATION?

You can submit to mediation at any time during the divorce process. After you receive a Complaint, you and your spouse may decide that mediation is the best way for you to negotiate a settlement. Or near the end of a divorce process, if it appears that you and your wife are headed to trial, you may choose mediation to avoid this situation. In most cases, however, mediators see people early in the divorce process. Most of them have friends who have been through brutal divorces. When they come into mediation, one of the motivations is to avoid this experience as well as the costly legal expenses of a divorce action.

37. WHAT IS THE COST OF MEDIATION?

Mediation is far less than attorney's fees—as much as 2/3 less. However, after a mediator has helped you negotiate an agreement, it should be reviewed by your attorney who must also file it with the court. After reviewing an agreement, some attorneys may say that they could have obtained a "better deal" for you. But at what cost? If it means months of unpleasant wrangling which undermines your relationship with your spouse and jeopardizes your efforts at being an effective parent following the divorce, is a "better deal" really worth it?

38. HOW DO YOU FIND AN EFFECTIVE MEDIATOR?

Much the same way that you find an attorney—you can rely on recommendations from friends. Then you should spend a little time interviewing several mediators. You'll know if you feel comfortable talking with them, face to face, and if they are really listening and responding to your concerns.

39. WHAT HAPPENS IN THE MEDIATION PROCESS?

One mediation team interviewed for this book explained that they begin mediation by explaining the process to the divorcing couple. Then they try to deal with financial issues, because "this brings reality into the situation." The team expects a husband and wife to assemble all the necessary information on their income, expenses, assets and liabilities—ideally they should do this work together—to determine what is realistic in terms of alimony and child support.

"Money is often limited," one of the team explains, "and

we have to determine how much a man can afford in child support, for example, and still retain enough financial resources to rent a large enough apartment to comfortably accommodate his children for visitations. This is a critical issue for a man who wants to continue being an involved father. If he can't afford to accommodate his children during visitations, it will be very difficult for him to do more than take them out on Sundays. And he becomes no more than a 'Santa Claus.'"

Usually, the team works with both spouses together. But each member may also take one of the spouses into a separate room and talk to him or her about any behavior which may be blocking progress toward an agreement. The team readily admits that they try to identify "hot" issues early and stay away from them until later in the mediation process. This enables the spouses to establish rapport and reach agreement in relatively broad areas so they can build momentum toward a final settlement. Then they have such a stake in the success of the process, that they are not likely to abandon it even when they must deal with especially difficult issues.

In mediation, the team explains, there shouldn't be any winners or losers. Each person must be prepared to compromise and give up some things and even be dissatisfied with certain parts of the agreement. No one should come out saying "I got a great deal!" That's not the spirit of mediation. Instead, they should come out believing it was fair to both of them.

> In mediation there shouldn't be any winners or losers.

40. ARE THERE CASES THAT SHOULD NOT BE SUBMITTED TO MEDIATION?

In cases where there is abuse, or one spouse is clearly afraid of the other, a lawyer may be necessary. Or if one spouse is very controlling and refuses to share any financial information, it is unlikely that this attitude will change in mediation. So the process will not work successfully.

41. WHAT TYPES OF CUSTODY ARRANGEMENTS ARE COMMON IN DIVORCE CASES?

In many cases women receive sole custody of their children—that is, the children reside with them and they have the legal right to make all the decisions affecting their lives. But in an increasing number of instances, the court supports the efforts of men and women who are agreeing to joint custody.

In some cases, joint custody means that children divide their time almost equally with each parent. This usually requires an enormous amount of cooperation between divorced parents, and very few of them are capable of getting along this well. In far more situations, the children continue to live with their mother, but both parents share responsibility for major decision-making. Some lawyers believe that this type of arrangement is worth fighting for because it gives both parents important input into their child's upbringing. Each parent now has a voice in a child's health care, for example, education and religion.

Other lawyers believe that joint custody is a facade. "You can't legislate cooperation," as one of them put it. If a woman is not getting along with her former husband, she can decide not to tell him when his children are going to the doctor and withhold any reports on their health. However, even without joint custody, men are still legally entitled to any information regarding the health and education of their children, at least in many states. They may have to contact the doctors and school officials themselves to obtain this information.

So don't be fooled into giving up something—such as significant equity in your house—to achieve joint custody. One man we interviewed gave away thousands of dollars to his wife after she threatened to kill his chances for joint custody if he didn't agree to her financial demands. Then she ignored the letter and the spirit of the agreement. Joint custody may not mean very much in the long run, and you still have legal rights even without it.

42. CAN A DIVORCE AGREEMENT BE CHANGED?

Some parts of an agreement cannot be changed, such as property settlements—who gets the house, etc. Alimony can be increased or reduced if your divorce agreement says that it is modifiable and circumstances change, such as the deterioration of your financial resources or the substantial improvement in your wife's finances. Child support payments can be changed for similar reasons. And the terms of your visitation schedule may also be modified as your children grow and a different schedule seems more appropriate.

While some parents may agree between themselves to be flexible when it comes to minor adjustments in visitation, as a general rule no major change in a divorce agreement should be made on your own. If you unilaterally decide to reduce your support payments, for example, your wife can have your paycheck garnished. Should both of you verbally agree to reduce her alimony, and she changes her mind later, she can force you to make back payments if a written agreement was not filed with the court and a modification wasn't legally made.

Your attorneys or mediator should negotiate the changes in the terms of your divorce, which must be put on the court record as a modification to the original judgment. If no out-of-court agreement is possible, then a hearing before a judge will be necessary.

CHAPTER IV

MAKING THE MOST OF VISITATIONS

Visitation is a word that's closely associated with divorce. Usually the father becomes the visiting parent, because the mother generally receives physical custody. This has begun changing, but only slowly. In a recent case in Washington, DC, for example, the judge awarded custody to the father who had spent more time with his children than his wife, a busy Congressional aide. But this decision is really the exception, that only proves the rule.

Visitation turns many fathers into little more than visitors to their children, which is the origin of the phrase "Uncle Dad". Yet it doesn't have to be that way. Instead of an insurmountable hurdle, a father can learn to vault over visitation and establish a close relationship with his children. But we would be kidding if we didn't tell you that it takes work and commitment. The process begins by trying to achieve a visitation schedule that is both realistic, based on the current demands you have on your time from a job, etc., as well as in the best interests of your kids. It also involves a realization that the visitation schedule will have to change as your kids mature, which may mean protracted negotiations with your ex-wife and possibly several trips to court. And if she moves out of state to remarry or begin a new job, the schedule will probably change again, requiring major readjustments in your lifestyle. It's all part of being a divorced father who wants to maintain a meaningful relationship with his kids

Visitations often become a battleground as ex-spouses find themselves arguing over all sorts of issues when a father arrives to pick-up his children. "I smile and bite my tongue," one man told us and it may be the best advice to follow when taking your children for a visit. Certainly, it's no time to get into an argument with their mother, which can only cast a bleak shadow over the entire visitation. Sometimes your wife may try to withhold the children and prevent you from seeing them during visitation. There are some ways for you to deal with this problem, but the best advice we can offer is try to prevent it from ever arising. Any serious conflict between you and your ex-wife will only have an adverse effect on your children.

43. WHAT KIND OF VISITATION SCHEDULE SHOULD YOU TRY TO ACHIEVE?

Your visitation schedule will be hammered out during negotiations between you and your spouse. She probably won't get everything that she wants, nor will you, so be prepared to compromise. Perhaps the best advice we can provide is for you to work out your top priorities before going into the negotiations.

1. Know what kind of visitation schedule you can actually keep. Don't be unrealistic. If you have a hectic career which

involves constant travel, you probably won't be able to adhere to a schedule that involves seeing your children two or three days during the week as well as part of every weekend. And once you begin missing visitations, you'll simply disappoint your kids and undermine your relationship with them. A traditional schedule of every other weekend may be more realistic for you. But you run a risk here, too. As one divorced Dad put it: "If you want to be a parent and not a visitor, you have to see your kids more than every other weekend."

2. Recognize what's in the best interests of your kids. This often creates a conflict with the first point. But if you want to be more than a "visitor", you must begin to understand the needs of your children. And this may require some changes in your current lifestyle. The frequency of visits often depends on the age of your child. Very young children, for example, need to see you more often to feel reassured that you have not abandoned them. The enormous upheaval which divorce causes in their lives can seem especially terrifying, and the father-child bond may be so fragile that it can break very easily. Therefore, short, frequent visits may be extremely important—even as often as an hour or two every other day.

Teenagers, on the other hand, may be so absorbed in their own lives that frequent visits will seem inappropriate. Frankly, they may prefer to be with their friends rather than spending time with either you or their mother. Nevertheless, we recommend that you try to develop a schedule that will bring you together with them more than the traditional every other weekend. You should try to see your children at least once during the week, for at least a breakfast or dinner, if not a sleep-over. And if you have more than one child, schedule some time when you can see each one individually—a child wants and needs this kind of special attention. Continuity and frequency are critical for a relationship to work. Otherwise too many things can occur in between visits, and by the time you see your children, it's too late to share what's happened in their busy lives.

44. CAN YOU CHANGE A VISITATION SCHEDULE?

Since children's needs change as they grow older, it's logical to assume that you will modify your schedule, too. You and your former wife should try to agree on these changes, then seek the approval of the court through your attorneys. Some divorced couples simply make an informal arrangement to change the visitation schedule, without consulting their lawyers, which may work out very smoothly. But we also know of situations where a woman has claimed later that she never agreed to any modification and uses this leverage to pry some other concession out of her former husband.

If a divorced couple cannot agree on a change in visitation, then they must go to court. (See Letters section.) To be successful in this arena, adequate preparation is extremely important. Talk to your attorney and make sure the modification makes sense. Discuss it with your children. If you can secure their agreement, then there's a good chance that the court will agree to it too. Nevertheless, the judge may defer a decision and order an investigation (by Family Relations, or a similar agency of the court) to determine whether a new visitation schedule is in the best interests of the children. This process may take six months or more. Therefore, if you want to readjust a visitation schedule to meet the changing needs of your child as he enters adolescence, it's often best to anticipate a delay and begin the procedure early.

As children grow older, they have the capacity to spend longer blocks of time with you. For example, you might consider having them for a complete school vacation during the winter, instead of only part of a week at that time, and a few days again over Spring Break. Or instead of every other weekend in the summer, you could decide to take the children for an entire month. While this arrangement may place more of a burden on a divorced father, who must dedicate longer and more concentrated periods of time to his children, it can immeasurably strengthen the bonds that tie your family together.

45. WHAT SHOULD YOU DO IF YOUR FORMER WIFE WANTS TO REDUCE YOUR VISITATION SCHEDULE?

Don't get angry, except privately. Then think about what your ex-wife is asking and decide whether it's really in the best interests of the children. If they're old enough, discuss the modification with them. You should be guided by their feelings, unless it dramatically reduces your time with them. That's counterproductive and may indicate some serious problem in your relationship with them that needs immediate attention. If you believe that your former wife is trying to wrest the children away from you, it's important to discuss this issue with her immediately. (See Letters section.) You should also emphasize to your kids how much you cherish the time you spend together so they won't easily be influenced by their mother and give it up. If all else fails, you may decide to consult your attorney and return to court, if necessary, to prevent a change in the visitation schedule.

46. WHAT CAN YOU DO IF YOUR EX-WIFE MOVES FAR AWAY?

If a woman decides to move out of state to begin a new job or to remarry, the court will most likely grant her request and there is nothing you can do to stop her. One man went to the community where his former wife and children relocated. He was a professional who could transfer his skills to a new geographical area, but most men can't. The sad realization that you won't be seeing your children as often as before can be extremely difficult to accept. As one man put it: "My son was so young, that if I had not seen him for a long period of time he might have forgotten who I was."

In this situation, you must do everything possible not to lose contact with your children. Call them regularly on the telephone, but at times which will not conflict with their favorite television program or homework schedule. And write frequently. "I wrote them postcards every week," a divorced father told us. "It was sometimes hard to think of things to write about. I would tell them how the garden was doing. Or I would tell them that I still had the picture they sent me which they made in school. I always tried to find something that they could relate to."

You should also be prepared to seek a modification in your visitation schedule. Since you can no longer see the children every week, request that they spend the entire summer vacation with you. Alternatively, they could be with you part of the summer, and part of the winter and spring school breaks. You might also consider spending one of your vacations near your children and having them with you. While any of these options may disrupt your lifestyle, a truly committed parent must be prepared to make these adjustments.

Distance is one of the most difficult barriers to overcome for a divorced father, and it often involves sacrifices. (Note: If you are offered a new job far away from your children, then you must decide whether to take it or remain where you are. The answer may depend on what kind of father you want to be now and in the future, as well as how you want your children to see you. Many men will take the new job, but they may be giving up a close relationship with their children. It's much harder to maintain this relationship at long distance. Our own view is that a man should live no farther than an hour from his children to maintain a regular visitation schedule.)

> **A truly committed parent must be prepared to make adjustments.**

47. HOW DO YOU PREVENT THE VISITATION FROM BECOMING A BATTLEGROUND?

Remember that the purpose of visitations is to pick up your children, not to argue with your ex-wife about any of the issues in your divorce agreement. If the visitation regularly becomes a battleground over issues such as alimony or whether she made the car payments on time, then your children may eventually decide that it's better to avoid the entire problem and they may refuse to go with you.

I used to get into battles with my ex-wife during visitations that irritated her, made me angry, and always upset my children. (Indeed, it was especially difficult for my son to make the transition from his mother's house to mine after an argument.) Finally, I wrote her a letter saying that when I arrived to pick up the kids, I would honk the horn twice and she could send them out to the car. When I returned with them, she could stand at the front door and I would send them in to her. To this day, I follow the same procedure so my former wife and I can avoid the face-to-face contact that might result in an argument.

It's often a good idea to call before you leave home and talk to your children or your ex-wife and let them know that you are on the way. One expert recommends that you write down what you want to say to your former wife and stick only to that topic, no matter what she says. If you have to alter your regular visitation schedule for any reason, make sure to tell your ex-wife as soon as possible. (See Letters section.) Doing anything less is not only very inconsiderate, these last minute changes are also a major cause of arguments that can undermine a pleasant visitation with your children.

48. WHAT CAN YOU DO IF YOUR EX-WIFE DOESN'T ABIDE BY THE LEGAL VISITATION SCHEDULE ?

Divorced Dads often tell us that their ex-wives hold the children as "hostages" to insure that they receive their child support payments or to wring out new concessions on other issues. So when it comes time for a father to pick up his kids, she may refuse to let them go with him. As one man put it: "I went to pick up my kids and my ex-wife and her new husband told me I couldn't have them. If I had contacted the police, they would have told me there was nothing they could do. So I went home and there was a message on my answering machine from her saying that she had reconsidered. Back I went to her house again, only to have her slam the door in my face. I never did get to see my children that weekend." That time was lost forever.

One way to deal with this frustrating situation is to involve a third party. Call the children's psychologist, or their lawyer if they have one, or the family relations counselor and ask them to call your ex-wife. She will then realize that someone else knows about the problem and can be called as a witness if you take the matter to court. This may force her to back off and allow you to see your kids.

You should also call your children and tell them what's happening. Explain that you want to see them but for reasons that you don't understand, their mother won't let you maintain your visitation schedule. Make sure that your children know how much you miss them and what efforts you are currently making to deal with the current problem. Otherwise, they may assume that you don't want to spend time with them.

(Note: We believe that you should do everything possible to keep peace with your ex-wife for the sake of the children. In some instances, however, she may act unfairly and you must be prepared to react accordingly. Nevertheless, we urge you to try reasoned discussions to resolve your conflicts before resorting to any other measures. If telephone conversations don't work, try writing her letters. These will give your ex-wife an opportunity to read what you want to say without the pressure of responding immediately. By escalating the conflict unnecessarily, you may only be jeopardizing your long-term relationship with your kids.)

49. HOW CAN YOU DEAL WITH A CHILD WHO DOESN'T WANT TO COME WITH YOU FOR A VISIT?

Don't take it personally. Some men are defeated too easily and they give up and go away. The reason may simply be that your child isn't feeling well and wants to stay home in her own bed or she may prefer to play with her friends that weekend. Try to understand what's going on and deal with it effectively.

Immediately following the divorce, my daughter, who was five years old at the time, didn't want to come with me. At first I felt devastated, fearing that she might never want to visit me. Finally, I convinced her to sit in the car and I told her that she didn't have to come to my home. I also explained my disappointment and asked if she might reconsider the next time. I had let my daughter off the hook, and she agreed to see me on the next visit. During the following week, I called my daughter more frequently and told her how much I was looking forward to spending time with her. This provided additional reassurance, and the visitation proceeded very smoothly.

If your son or daughter repeatedly refuses to go with you, the reason may be a far more serious one. Sometimes you can persuade the child to talk about it, if he is old enough. Perhaps the problem lies with something that happened during a previous visit. Or it may be caused by your ex-wife who is trying to prevent the child from seeing you. The best way to handle this situation is to talk to your ex-wife and attempt to resolve the situation.

LETTERS

Dear (former wife):

I read your response to my request to have the children for dinner on alternate Sundays of the weekends they are not with me. I'm writing once again in hopes we can resolve this issue to avoid filing a motion with the court.

You know the importance of each child having separate time with me on Tuesdays. Both of them look forward to this "one to one" time when I can focus on them alone. Suggesting that this part of my visitation schedule be eliminated in favor of the dinners on Sundays would not be in the best interests of the children.

I know you understand the importance of the children seeing me. For this reason I again propose eliminating alternate Friday breakfasts, which was in our original visitation schedule, for alternate Sunday dinners. Fridays have become impractical because highway construction prevents me from picking up the children early enough for breakfast. In addition, my job is requiring more early morning meetings, which often fall on Friday.

I'm not requesting additional time, only a logical improvement of the schedule. I'd very much like to avoid filing a motion to achieve this change.

Dear (former wife),

As we both must realize after almost three years of joint custody, flexibility (within reason) is needed at times. Within the spirit of cooperation, we are committed to the agreements made in the divorce document.

I am entitled to a half hour flexibility when picking up the children for a visitation. You have no right to demand that I be there at 5 P.M. sharp or "no one would be there." I'm driving thirty miles!

If on any given pick-up day your schedule requires me to be at your house at a specific time between 4:30 and 5:30, I'll really try to accommodate you. This is in the spirit of compromise and flexibility. But when you demand "I better be there or else," I'll be forced to refer to the divorce agreement.

Please try to cooperate with me for the sake of the children. As you know by now, I'm not going to fade away. It's in all our best interests to cooperate, especially in the area of schedules.

Dear (former wife),

I'd like to confirm the children's visitation schedule with me for the coming few months. If you have any problems, please let me know.

Tuesday, June 24 Son—dinner/overnight
Friday, June 27 Children/weekend
Tuesday, July 1 Daughter—dinner/overnight
Friday, July 4 Children/breakfast
Tuesday, July 8 Son—dinner/overnight
Friday, July 11 Children/weekend
Tuesday, July 15 Daughter—dinner/overnight
Friday, July 18 Children/breakfast
Tuesday, July 22 Son—dinner/overnight
Friday, July 25 Children/2 weeks summer vacation
Sunday, August 10 Children—dinner
Tuesday, August 12 Daughter—dinner/overnight
Friday, August 15 Children/breakfast
Tuesday, August 19 Son—dinner/overnight
Friday, August 22 Children/weekend
Tuesday, August 26 Daughter—dinner/overnight

Dear (former wife),

As we discussed a few weeks ago, I want to remind you that next weekend, June 13-15, I'll be returning the children to you on Sunday. Originally I said I would return them at 5 p.m. But I now realize it must be at 4 p.m. in order to catch a flight. I hope this one hour change won't be a problem. If it means you needing a sitter, I'd be happy to pay for it.

Dear (former wife),

Now that your move is a reality, I'd like to propose some changes in the visitation schedule. These would make life easier on the children, and on me since I must drive farther now to pick them up or take them to school. I sincerely hope we are at the stage where we can deal with these minor changes without having to consult with lawyers. It's in the best interests of the children, and you and me if we can resolve these issues on our own.

Please let me know how you feel about the following modification of the current visitation schedule 1. On the weekends I have the children, I return them to you Sunday evenings at 7 P.M. (after dinner) instead of bringing them to their appropriate schools on Monday mornings. 2. Since the driving distance will prohibit me from having the children for alternate breakfasts on Fridays, can I have them for dinner or dessert on the Sunday evenings of the weekends I don't have the children? This way we won't go seven to ten days without seeing each other.

Please consider these changes in a spirit of cooperation concerning the best interests of the children. I want to continue being as active in their lives as I have been the past two years. Please think this proposal over. I await to hear from you.

CHAPTER V

A HOME AWAY FROM HOME

Creating a warm, comfortable home for yourself and your children should be a top priority for every divorced Dad. A significant element of any home environment is the emotional climate that you establish there. Instead of trying to spend each hour in endless activity, as many divorced fathers try to do, it's far more important to build in a significant amount of unstructured time with your children so you can find out about all the things that are happening in their world. Listening is an essential skill in building a supportive environment for your kids. They also need an open demonstration of your affection—not once in awhile, but repeatedly—to reassure themselves during the turmoil of a divorce that you still love them. Bath time and bedtime can be excellent opportunities to bond with your young children. By singing songs or reading bedtime stories to your kids, you can immeasurably enrich your relationship with them, even during the limited time available to you during a visitation. Your children will also benefit from any activities you can share together—whether it's cooking, playing games or attending sporting events. Each one provides a special chance to bond with them.

Another way to strengthen the bonds between you and your children is to create a physical environment in your home that makes them feel welcome. Let your children help decorate their own room, encourage them to bring their friends to visit and even spend the night, and put their papers from school on your refrigerator to show that you're proud of their accomplishments. Of course, children may also need your guidance to perform to their full potential in the classroom, so it's essential to set firm guidelines regarding homework. Provide a quiet well-lighted area where they can work and be sure they know that you expect them to use it.

Vacations and holidays can become special occasions for you and your children, without spending a bundle of money. You don't need to buy your children's affections with expensive Hannukah/Christmas presents and lavish trips, if you've been a nurturing and affectionate parent during the rest of the year. This not only includes visitation periods, but the days when you're apart from each other. Letters, cards and telephone calls can enable you to stay in touch with your children even when you don't see them.

Remember, children want a Dad 365 days a year. While it's often more difficult to satisfy their needs as a visiting father, you can still succeed if you're willing to make the commitment.

50. HOW DO YOU PREPARE FOR A VISITATION WITH YOUR CHILDREN?

A divorced father has often been compared to Santa

Claus—a man who attempts to fill each visitation with exciting entertainment, exotic trips or lavish gifts. Why do so many divorced fathers seem to fall into the Santa Claus syndrome? One reason may be that fathers often lose touch with their children between visitations. Instead of trying to reestablish communication during a visitation, it is frankly much easier to keep the children as busy as possible going places and buying things. Many men may also feel guilty about the divorce and to assuage these feelings they decide to indulge their children, never stopping to ask whether this is really what's best for them.

It isn't. Nor is endless entertaining an effective way to build a relationship. While it's important to do some planning for a visitation, it's enough to plan only one or two activities with your children. Don't over-plan. You need quiet time for family interaction, which usually takes place around mundane events like grocery shopping, cleaning the house, doing homework, or reading together. Many men become anxious during these quiet times. But they provide you with an opportunity to be yourself and for your kids to be themselves, too. It also gives them a chance to talk and for you to listen.

If you want to find out what's really happening in your children's lives, the key is listening. Children love to talk about themselves, to tell you what they've been doing since the last time you've seen them, to hear your reactions to their successes and even their failures. But this process requires time to just hang out together. It will never happen if you're busy running from one spectacular event to the next in an effort to keep your children busy.

Frenzied activity only builds barriers, it can never build

relationships.

51. HOW DO YOU ESTABLISH A COMFORTABLE ENVIRONMENT FOR YOUR CHILDREN?

When you select an apartment or house in which to live, try to consider the needs of your children. Is the neighborhood safe? Are there families and children in the area with whom your kids can play? Are there activities nearby, such as movies, parks, zoos, etc.?

One divorced father we interviewed selected an apartment complex on a dead-end street so his kids would have a safe place to ride their bicycles. He also made sure there were other children in the building as well as a local park a short distance away.

If your children have their own room in your new home, they should be given a major role in decorating it. This enables them to feel that the room is really their own. Involve them as much as possible in choosing furniture or selecting pictures for the walls. If you have more than one child and can't afford an apartment big enough for a room for each of them, then divide the single room to give the children their own space. One man used a large dresser as a divider and allowed his kids to decorate the walls on each side of the dresser to their own taste.

My first apartment was so small that the children didn't even have a single room to divide. At first I felt badly about it, but eventually I came up with the idea of turning the entire experience into a camp out for them. They slept on the floor in my room tucked inside their own cozy sleeping bags. It's a fond memory they still talk about to this day.

In addition to providing a room for your children (if you can afford one), try to make other parts of your home child-friendly. Decorate your refrigerator with papers which your children have done in school—artwork, tests, etc. This tells them how proud you are of their accomplishments and says to visitors that this is a place where children—outstanding children—are living. You might also have special chairs for them in the living room, so they will feel comfortable there, as well.

52. HOW DO YOU DEAL WITH YOUR CHILDREN'S FRIENDS?

Simple. Make their friends feel welcome when they're with you. Your children may express a desire to have their friends visit or spend the night during a visitation. To make this process as smooth as possible, you should get to know their parents so they will feel comfortable allowing their children to go with you. During some visitations, your children may wish to spend time with friends at their homes. This may involve considerable driving, leaving the children off for several hours, and finding activities to keep yourself busy until you pick them up again. Don't try to economize on driving. Divorce and visitation only increase the amount of chauffeuring you'll be called upon to do as a parent. You'll have to get used to being on call to pick up your children from their mother's house (which may be an hour or more away), taking them to play in sports or other events, and then calling for them when they're ready. As a parent, your time is often not your own.

53. WHAT KIND OF LIFESTYLE SHOULD YOU CREATE FOR YOURSELF AS A SINGLE PARENT?

The best answer is one that balances your needs with the needs of your children. But that's not an easy balance to strike.

Following my divorce, I immersed myself in the children. I felt guilty because of my role in causing the divorce and wanted to make up for it with my kids. So I tried to become a super Dad. While this may have been helpful to building a relationship with them, it also prevented me from becoming a whole person. Finally, I realized that I didn't have to dote on them all the time, which left me free to develop a relationship with a wonderful woman who has been my significant other for many years. As time passed and our love became stronger, she has contributed significantly to the sense of family that all of us now share.

Some men, of course, are so dependent on a relationship to ward off the loneliness in their lives, that they are apt to pursue the first attractive woman who comes along. And a short time later, they may even marry again. Unfortunately an even higher percentage of these second marriages result in divorce than first ones.

Most men need to spend time alone to find out who they are and learn to like themselves. Give yourself a chance to read, pursue your hobbies, or develop new interests. These are the types of activities where you are likely to find someone—

someone with whom you're most compatible. These people are not apt to be sitting on bar stools in pick-up joints surrounded by a group of hungry men.

Initially, I was alone for several months following my divorce. When I finally began dating, women were often introduced to be me by friends. While these women were very pleasant, the relationships really didn't lead anywhere. Finally when I met my current significant other, I had a much better idea of the type of woman with whom I felt most comfortable. I had also overcome much of my mistrust of women and felt prepared to make a long-term commitment to a relationship.

54. HOW DO YOU BECOME A NURTURER AND BOND WITH YOUR CHILDREN DURING A SHORT VISITATION?

It doesn't come easily for men to demonstrate affection for their children. But this is the key to creating a strong bond with them and building a deep, nurturing relationship. Don't be afraid to hug your children frequently and let them know how much you love them—they can never hear these words too often. Children also want you to be open to their hugs and kisses. There's no limit on affection; encourage it and it will enrich your life.

Not only should you be a nurturer, rely also on relatives— aunts, uncles and grandparents—to provide your children with love and understanding. Following a divorce, these people are now more important than ever in providing your children with a sense of family.

55. WHAT ROLE CAN BATHS AND BEDTIME STORIES PLAY IN BONDING WITH YOUNG CHILDREN?

If you have young children, bath time can be a wonderful opportunity for nurturing and communication. Don't just run their bath, help them into it and walk away—that certainly won't bring you any closer to your kids. Instead, sit down in the bathroom, watch your children play with their toys and wait for them to strike up a conversation. You'll be surprised at how much they tell you about their day, their friends, their school work, and how often they provide some incisive as well as amusing comments on world (their world) affairs.

While it's helpful if you can participate in the discussion, your most important role is to be a good listener. Children want very badly for you to listen to them—it's another way of showing your affection.

When my daughter was only four, I began singing her three songs at bedtime. Eight years later, she still found my singing a comforting and reassuring way to help her fall asleep. Indeed, I'm confident she will one day sing these same songs to her children!

My son, on the other hand, preferred the bedtime stories I used to tell him. When he was seven, I invented a fictitious character named Timmy and for almost three years he enjoyed hearing about Timmy's adventures. Once, when I had to undergo surgery and couldn't be at home for a month, I simply recorded some new episodes of Timmy's story on tape so he could listen to them each night at bedtime.

Bedtime is an excellent opportunity to bond with your children and nurture your relationship with them. No matter how bad your voice may be, learn to sing a few songs to your children before they go to sleep. This will help them relax and feel secure. You might also consider taping the songs so your children can listen to them when they are not visiting you.

(Incidentally, your singing need not be restricted to a child's bedtime. When he was a baby, my son loved to hear me sing to him in the car. In fact, it often was the only way to stop him from crying on long trips. He particularly enjoyed a Mozart piece which I hummed to him over and over again. Finally, out of sheer exhaustion, I decided to make a tape recording of it. I kept playing and replaying the tape on car trips and he never knew the difference.)

One of the best ways of strengthening the relationship between you and your children is by reading to them at bedtime. This enables you to sit close to each other and share some quiet moments together at the end of the day. Children love to listen to a story, look at the pictures, ask questions and allow their imaginations to roam. They also appreciate the fact that the story is being read to them by you. Many appropriate books are available at your local library. Indeed, a very enjoyable way for you and your children to spend time together is at the library looking for stories that they would like to hear. As they grow older, children will want to read their own books. Encourage them to read and help them make selections.

56. WHAT ROLE SHOULD YOU PLAY IN HELPING YOUR CHILDREN WITH THEIR HOMEWORK?

Homework is critically important to a child's success in school. However, it can easily fall through the cracks as he bounces back and forth between you and your former spouse, dealing with all the distractions frequent travel inevitably entails and adjusting to different environments.

Be sure to set aside a well lighted area so your kids realize where they can do homework without feeling that it's someone else's space. Create an area that they know is theirs, but not far out of eye or ear contact with you. You should also set down some hard and fast rules governing homework to insure that your children actually accomplish their assignments when they are at your home. From our interviews with divorced men, we've discovered that this is often an area of conflict with their ex-wives. As one man put it: "She thinks I'm too tough on my son because I want him to do too much homework." But a woman also told us that she always has to play the role of the "heavy" because her ex-husband is far too lenient in enforcing the rules regarding homework.

It's especially important for you and your former wife to be consistent when it comes to homework, otherwise your children may question your commitment to it. Therefore, it's critical that you discuss homework rules with her and settle on the same approach to this issue. (See Letters section.)

57. HOW DO YOU FIND ACTIVITIES TO SHARE WITH YOUR CHILDREN?

Listen and they'll let you know. What's more, you will no longer need to feel responsible for everyone's good times, which removes an enormous burden from your shoulders. Instead of playing Santa Claus, you only need to be Dad. And, like any Dad, you and your children will have many interests in common and activities you can share together—whether it's reading, music, nature, or even baseball.

When I was growing up baseball was not just a sport, it was a way of life. My father and I pursued the game from early April to October, and my mother suffered the fate of trying to keep her son's uniforms clean. I was a catcher, spending thirteen consecutive summers on the sandlot fields of Brooklyn, New York. But sometime between the ages of 18 and 19 I realized, like thousands of young men, that my "career" was coming to an end. All the dreams and fantasies had to be put aside for the real life goals of college and beyond.

Just when I thought my fervor for the game was comfortably tucked away (except for the Fall Classic) my son began to show an enthusiastic interest in baseball, rekindling all those intense and wonderful feelings which I thought were gone forever. We played ball together, we went to professional games, and I cheered from the sidelines at my son's own games until I thought my lungs would break.

In addition to playing baseball, my son found a way to avoid hanging up his cleats and glove for our cold New England winters through another hobby we've both learned to appreciate: collecting baseball cards. My son's collection now totals over 12,000 cards as well as autographed baseballs, programs, and pictures. Our greatest interest is the "Bums" of Brooklyn—Jackie Robinson, Duke Snyder and all the other Dodger greats. I'm also amazed how much my son knows about the other players, managers, owners, and ballparks of the 1940s and 1950s. He has long ago surpassed me in his knowledge of those decades—years I was living or dying with every Dodger win or loss and devastated after each Brooklyn World Series defeat at the hands of those miserable Yankees. This common interest enabled us to develop an even stronger father/son relationship. (See Letters section.)

58. WHAT TYPES OF ACTIVITIES SHOULD YOU PLAN FOR THEM?

Keep it simple and don't over-plan. Be prepared to take advantage of unforeseen opportunities. For example, if a child is having a problem with a science project, the best way to deal with it might be a trip to the local museum which can take up half the day. Raking the leaves is an activity that can be turned into a contest between your kids to determine who's the best raker—with a small prize going to the winner and, of course, a consolation for the runner up. Or a game like Scrabble™ or Monopoly™ can keep you and your kids occupied for the entire afternoon. While some kids might prefer to sit in front of the television or play computer games, we discourage too much of this kind of activity because it doesn't provide as much opportunity for you and your children to interact.

Another way to spend the day is to suggest that your kids invite their friends over to the house for a game of basketball or baseball. There might also be some other children living in your neighborhood who could join in this activity. The essential goal in all of these undertakings is to create a family environment. Instead of focusing on the negative aspects of divorce, especially the fact that you and your kids no longer live in an intact family, overcome this problem as so many other single-parent families do—by making the best of the situation as they find it. You may feel overwhelmed and a little exhausted most of the time. But somehow everything will get done.

Remember, you only have the children for a few days each month. It's not much time put up with a little extra confusion in your life. And it's usually worth it just to be with them.

59. WHY SHOULD YOU LEARN TO BE A BETTER COOK?

If you're already a good cook, terrific. But if your ex-wife did most of the cooking, then it's important for you to learn how to make a few healthy and tasty meals to serve your children when they're with you for the weekends. This doesn't mean learning much more than four or five recipes, because your kids aren't with you all the time. I quickly discovered several ways to cook chicken as well as how to prepare some simple pasta dishes. If you're a poor cook, you can always seek help from family, friends or cookbooks. A series which is especially helpful is *365 Ways to Cook*. These include books on cooking chicken, pasta, beef, etc.

We strongly recommend that you eat out less and cook in more. It's cost effective, and a great way to nurture the relationship with your kids. Try to plan special meals and allow your kids to help in the preparation and cooking responsibilities, or at least in setting the table. One man told us that his children often couldn't agree on the dinner they wanted, so he put several choices on pieces of paper, folded them, and had the kids pick one out of a hat. While this approach may sound somewhat artificial, it's another way to involve your children in mealtime preparation and make regular meals a special occasion.

You can also take the kids along on your trips to the grocery store to do the shopping. This is a task that most men don't enjoy anyway, and a few helping hands can make it go much faster. Let the children participate in meal planning for the weekends, or if they spend a night with you during the week, ask them to help you select the foods to include in their lunch box for the next day.

Always try to prepare a school lunch for your children even if they return to their mother's house on a Sunday evening after your visitation. They can put the lunch in the refrigerator and take it to school on Monday morning. A nice touch is to add a note in the lunch bag saying something such as: "Have a great day! I look forward to seeing you next on _____. Love, Dad."

Since time is limited during visitations, you should make every effort to use the hours spent with your kids as creatively and constructively as possible.

60. HOW DO YOU HANDLE THE HOLIDAY SEASON?

For many divorced Dads, the holiday season can be a time of considerable sadness. If you've been accustomed to spending Christmas or Hanukkah with your family and now you're living alone, it can only magnify the sense of loss associated with divorce. It may also be painful for you to see those Dads in intact families happily celebrating the season with their kids. Somehow the days and weeks from Thanksgiving through Christmas only seem to magnify your failures and reinforce your sense of loneliness.

According to some visitation schedules, divorced fathers can see their children either for Thanksgiving or Christmas, but not both. Other schedules may allow you part of each holiday with your kids. This makes it difficult to create a meaningful celebration with your children, and it's easy to fall back into the Santa syndrome to compensate for your feelings of guilt and frustration. If you're a Dad who can't afford to shower your children with gifts, the experience may be even more frustrating.

The best way to handle the holiday season is to recognize up front that it's a potentially emotional time. Don't try to compete with your former wife at Christmas or Hannukkah for the title of champion gift giver. If you've developed a meaningful relationship with your kids during the rest of the year, a simple celebration with a few presents should be more than enough to underscore the quality of your commitment to each other.

Some flexibility may also be required in your holiday

celebrations. For example, you may prefer to open presents on Christmas Eve rather than the next day. However, if your visitation schedule calls for your ex-wife to have the children on Christmas Eve, you must adjust to this situation.

The holiday season is often an occasion to take stock of our lives. If Christmas with your children does not prove to be everything you want, perhaps it's time to talk honestly with yourself about the reason for your disappointment. Is it just this one day that didn't turn out the way you wanted? Or is there a more serious problem in the relationship that you have established with your children? Holidays are traditionally an opportunity for making new resolutions, and what better one than improving your commitment and performance as a Dad?

61. HOW SHOULD YOU PLAN VACATIONS WITH YOUR KIDS?

The most effective approach is to look for places that provide a balance of activities for adults and young people. Be sure to ask your kids what they would enjoy on a vacation and try to satisfy their desires, if these options are financially possible.

Many men, however, cannot afford to take their children away on vacations after paying monthly alimony and/or child support. If you must stay at home with your kids for a week, creativity becomes extremely important. Begin planning a month or two in advance and involve your kids in the decision-making. The week may involve several trips to local movie theaters, a visit to a nearby zoo or sea aquarium, a picnic on the beach during the summer, or back-to-school shopping if the vacation occurs near the beginning of fall.

Let's face it, a week alone with the kids has the potential of driving a man to the insane asylum unless he plans adequately for it in advance. Don't feel that the entire responsibility must be yours alone because your kids want a say in it, too. And remember what we said about being able to just hang out with your children—it goes for vacations as well as the rest of the year. Vacations can be an opportunity instead of a burden—an opportunity to strengthen the bonds that tie you and your kids together. If you use it this way, the week will fly by instead of dragging along as so many vacations seem to do.

62. WHAT DOES YOUR CHILD WANT FROM YOU AS A VISITING PARENT?

If you're handling the situation well, your child will never see you as the visiting parent. Your child will see you as Dad. This must be your goal from the day you leave the house. When you accomplish it, then you know that you're handling the visitation schedule effectively and successfully fulfilling your role as a father. Your children should always think of you as Dad even when you're not with them. This will happen if you constantly stay in touch with your kids through letters, phone calls and visitations every week. (See Letters section.)

Men need to rediscover the art of letter writing. I've always sent my kids funny looking cards and written them letters during the days when I'm away from them. Everyone loves to get letters in the mail, and your kids are no exception. Write them letters about the little things that have happened to you during the week and ask them to write back about the events in their lives.

You should also plan to talk to your kids on the telephone as often as possible. This enables you to stay in touch during the days when you don't see them. The problem for most men is that too much is occurring in your children's lives between visitations, and it's too difficult to catch up when you only see them every other weekend. Children live in the moment and want to discuss what's happening to them as soon as it happens. If you're not there, the opportunity is lost. Since you can't be with your children all the time, the only way to make up for this situation is through regular use of the telephone and by sending frequent cards and letters.

LETTERS

Dear (former wife),

I'm hopeful we can agree to hiring a tutor for our son. I'd like to discuss this with you.

Personally I feel that 1-11/2 hours per week would be very important to him while not infringing upon his summer vacation. Logistically, I'm willing to work out any reasonable arrangement with you. Of course, I'll split the cost with you. Please let me know your thoughts on this matter.

Dear (son),

Wasn't it great going to our first baseball card show together! I just know this will be a hobby we can enjoy for many years to come. Those Brooklyn Dodger cards bring back so many good memories I shared with Grandpa. Now it's our turn. I look forward to seeing you and your sister on Friday for the weekend.

Dear (daughter),

I really enjoyed having dinner with you last night and watching the movie together. I hope you have a wonderful two weeks at camp. I'm sure you will make some new friends. Have a great time and I will write to you again.

Hi! (daughter)

It rained very hard last night and I thought of you all snug and cozy in your bunk. I bet you and your bunk mates had your flashlights going. I'm so glad you enjoy camp so much. Have you gone horseback riding?

Have fun and I'll write you again tomorrow.

Dear (daughter),

Hope your first week of camp has been a terrific one! I bet next week will be better yet. I spoke with Grandma yesterday. She said she will be writing to you and looks forward to taking you and your friend Michelle to her house in August. That's only a couple of weeks away!

We all wish you a great time and can't wait to see you next weekend.

You'll be sleeping over on Saturday night.

Dear (daughter),

It was such a good weekend together. I'm so glad you like your new bed. It certainly makes you cozy. On your next weekend visit, Grandma will be here.

She can't wait to see you—as always.

Have a wonderful week.

CHAPTER VI

THE CHALLENGE OF PARENTING

The growth of your children presents new challenges for every divorced father. One of the most difficult issues facing you and your ex-wife is trying to set consistent standards, especially if you're not communicating regularly with each other. Unfortunately, children may attempt to exploit this situation and try "to get away with something" when they're with one parent that they know the other would never allow.

While it may be very tempting for divorced couples to openly criticize each other's parenting skills in front of their children, this behavior only puts them in the middle. If you have a gripe with your ex-wife over the way she is raising your child, talk over the problem on the telephone or write her a letter.

Sometimes parent-teacher conferences or other school events can create conflicts between you and your ex-wife. But these problems can be avoided with a little advanced planning. Safeguarding your child's health can also become a battleground if your former wife prevents you from becoming involved in important health care decisions. However, you can remedy this situation by talking to your children's doctor and expressing your concern about their medical care.(See Letters Section.)

A child's physical and emotional well-being should always be your primary consideration. This means building a supportive family environment with the help of grandparents, aunts and uncles; making your children and their friends feel welcome at your home; and, most importantly, striking the proper balance between the demands of your job and your responsibilities as a divorced father.

63. HOW DO YOU AND YOUR EX-WIFE MAINTAIN A CONSISTENT APPROACH TO RAISING CHILDREN?

One man told us that he and his former wife have never been able to maintain a coordinated approach to child rearing because of their inability to communicate very successfully. Over the years they've paid a heavy price for this problem with their daughter who learned to "play off" one of them against the other while she was a child and has intensified this behavior during adolescence.

This man's daughter figured out very early how to manipulate a system in which two parents are not getting along and both are doing their own thing. For example, when the man tried to hold his daughter responsible for certain minimal tasks like cleaning her room or maintaining reasonable study habits in school, she rebelled. And her mother refused to enforce these minimal standards.

Perhaps, this girl had been angry at both her mother and father for many years because they divorced and didn't provide her with a traditional two-parent home. And she learned to express her anger by manipulating her parents. Unfortunately, she has never resolved these feelings. In fact, her hostility toward her parents has only increased due to the normal upheaval of adolescence, and her father's unwillingness to give in to her irresponsible behavior.

Is there any way to avoid this type of problem? Perhaps if the man and his wife had sought mediation when their divorce began, they could have maintained a smoother relationship with each other. This might have enabled them to communicate more effectively so they could have provided a coordinated approach to raising their child.

Many divorced couples try to practice what is called <u>co-parenting</u>. Both parents hope to cooperate as much as possible with each other to maintain consistency in their child rearing efforts. But co-parenting requires regular communication to work successfully. Unfortunately, couples often discover that they can't communicate about their children or any other issue without serious conflict. So they stop talking to each other. As a result, they find themselves engaged in <u>parallel parenting</u>—both parents do their own thing, which may be quite different. This leaves the children feeling uncertain over what is expected of them, and sometimes they may begin to manipulate the situation to their own advantage.

We cannot emphasize too strongly that you should do everything possible to keep open the channels of communication with your ex-wife, at least on matters that pertain to your children. As one divorced man told us: "As long as we keep the discussion on the kids, we're fine. We don't talk about anything else." He treats each discussion almost like a business transaction, which enables him to leave his emotions out of it. For this man and his ex-wife, the top priority is always the interests of their children. So they deal with each other civilly, at least in this one area.

64. WHAT SHOULD YOU DO IF YOUR EX-WIFE IS CRITICIZING YOU TO YOUR CHILDREN?

Perhaps the best course of action is to call your former wife and find out why she is making negative statements about you. If a telephone conversation is too painful or volatile, write her a letter.

No matter how you decide to communicate, try to avoid a confrontational tone with her because it will only add fuel to the fire. What's more, she may have a legitimate reason for finding fault with your behavior. Nevertheless, you should explain to your ex-wife that by criticizing your actions to the children, it only hurts them. Since they feel a loyalty to both of their parents, she is only putting them in the middle, making them feel anxious and insecure.

There is no guarantee, of course, that this method of dealing with the problem will work. Your former wife may continue criticizing you openly, and you may be forced to accept it. One divorced father explained: "I no longer worry about things that I can't control. Once you move out, you don't have control. It hurts, but that's the way it is." Your only recourse is to continue being a good father and trust that your kids will recognize how much you're doing for them.

65. SHOULD YOU EVER CRITICIZE YOUR EX-WIFE IN FRONT OF YOUR CHILDREN?

Ideally, never. But all of us do it. For example, one man told us that if his children resist when he wants them to complete their homework, he'll ask if they "get away" without doing it at their mother's house. This is meant as a subtle criticism of her. He'll also question them about whether they're eating their meals on time—another area where he and his ex-wife have different standards. In part, he's genuinely concerned about his children's well-being. But he is also trying to imply to them that he's a better parent than his ex-wife.

While all of us fall into these bad habits occasionally, other men seem to go much too far. Many of them are especially frustrated because, as our interviews have revealed, they believe that their ex-wives are "holding the children hostage for money." And they don't hesitate to criticize them openly for it. For instance, if a child wants to go to an amusement park, a man might say: "I can't afford it because of all the money I send to your mother." Child support is a fact of life, no matter how onerous it may seem to you. Nor are your children responsible for the amount of support you're required to pay.

If you find yourself repeatedly criticizing your ex-wife in front of your children over child support or anything else, you owe them an apology. It need not occur immediately after the incident. In fact, many men don't realize that they said anything that may be hurtful to their children until they reflect on it later. After you've had time to think, tell your kids that you made a mistake and shouldn't have said such things. Then try to prevent yourself from openly criticizing your former wife again.

66. HOW DO YOU ENSURE THAT TEACHERS KEEP YOU INFORMED OF YOUR CHILD'S SCHOOL WORK?

In many states, schools are mandated by law to give every parent their children's report cards as well as any other important notices regarding their academic and extracurricular activities. If your ex-wife withholds this information, be sure that the school principal knows who you are and that your address appears on the school's mailing list. In addition, I introduced myself each year to my children's teachers. I also provided self-addressed stamped envelopes to them so they could keep me informed of all significant events. In this way, I could keep abreast of everything that was happening in school and attend any important functions. (See Letters section.)

67. IF YOUR EX-WIFE DOESN'T TELL YOU ABOUT YOUR CHILD'S HEALTH PROBLEMS, HOW DO YOU OBTAIN THIS INFORMATION?

Like your children's school, their doctor may be required to provide you with any medical information pertaining to them.

Whether your child is going to a dentist for a routine examination or being treated by a pediatrician for a serious illness, you should know about it. If your ex-wife doesn't inform you of any medical procedures being performed on your son or daughter, be prepared to take the initiative and contact the doctor yourself. (See Letters section.) Unfortunately, many men disappear after a divorce so a doctor may assume that you are not concerned about the health of your children. Don't be afraid to give the physician a gentle reminder that you want to be involved in their health care. Then, plan to attend the medical appointment and talk to the doctor yourself about your child's condition.

68. HOW DO YOU PREPARE FOR A PARENT-TEACHER CONFERENCE WITH YOUR EX-WIFE?

Some men maintain such a smooth relationship with their ex-wives that both of them can attend a parent-teacher conference together and calmly discuss their child's performance in school. But if you're afraid that a conference might turn into a conflict with your former spouse, you should plan to talk to your child's teachers separately.

When your child is experiencing a problem in school, for example, it does no good for you and your ex-wife to start an argument and blame each other in front of the teacher. By talking to him on your own, you can have a meaningful exchange of ideas, and even develop an action plan to deal with the problem. You can also demonstrate to the teacher your strong commitment to the child's success in school.

Other activities such as school plays or athletic events can turn into awkward situations unless you plan for them. Suppose your son is performing in a play on the Friday evening of your visitation weekend. And, after the performance has ended your ex-wife asks him to go with her for an ice cream cone. What should you do? Say "no" and create a scene? Agree to let your son go with his mother while you wait around for an hour or more?

The most effective way to deal with this awkward situation is to anticipate it so you're not taken by surprise. Talk to your son during the week and agree on a way to handle the problem that will be acceptable to both of you.

Perhaps your daughter is participating in an extracurricular activity at a time which is not part of your visitation. It may feel uncomfortable for you to attend and see your ex-wife there, knowing that your daughter will go home with her and not with you. But, remember how important it is for that child to see you among the spectators. After the event is over, congratulate your daughter, give her a hug and explain that you're looking forward to seeing her during the next visitation. It only takes a few minutes, but it will mean so much to her.

69. WHY SHOULD YOU GET TO KNOW THE PARENTS OF YOUR CHILD'S FRIENDS?

As your children grow, they'll inevitably desire to spend more and more time with their friends, even during visitations with you. One way to deal with this sensitive situation is to invite these friends to visit your home. But this will only happen if their parents know who you are and feel comfortable permitting their children into your home.

Perhaps you've already met some of these parents at your child's school functions. But others may be strangers to you— even though your children and theirs have become close friends. The next time you take your son or daughter to visit these children, introduce yourself to their parents and talk with them for awhile. This will "break the ice". After additional meetings, you might suggest that their children come over to your home for a visit.

70. HOW DO YOU MAKE YOUR CHILD'S FRIENDS FEEL WELCOME AT YOUR HOME?

The best advice we can give is to demonstrate your interest in these children as soon as they arrive. First, you might show them where they're going to sleep. Don't worry if your apartment isn't big enough for them to have their own room or even their own bed.

Sleeping bags on the floor are more than adequate. This arrangement certainly worked for my children and their friends. Indeed, they sometimes took the floor and gave their friends the bed.

Ask your child's friends if there are any foods that they particularly like to eat. And suggest that they accompany you to the supermarket to shop for them. They may even decide to help you with the cooking.

It's unnecessary to plan any special events for your child's friends. They will usually stay busy with their own activities, as children usually do, or they can join you in the regular projects that are part of any normal visitation weekend. The most important thing is to let these children know that you enjoy having them stay at your home and appreciate the fact that your child has them as friends.

71. WHAT ROLE CAN GRANDPARENTS AND OTHER RELATIVES PLAY IN HELPING RAISE YOUR KIDS?

Ask any single parent, and they'll tell you that a support system is essential in helping them raise their children. During the early days of a divorce when you may feel uncertain of your parenting skills, grandparents can be invaluable, lending you a helping hand with baby sitting as well as various household chores. Although my mother had always enjoyed a close relationship with my kids, she spent even more time with them following the divorce. This enabled me to continue doing the traveling that was a necessary part of my job and even take brief vacations. I needed these short respites to recharge my batteries.

Your brothers and sisters can also form an integral part of a support network, especially if they have their own children. Exchange visits as often as you can and try to strengthen the relationship between your kids and their cousins. A child's extended family can often provide the continuity he needs during the upheaval of divorce.

72. HOW DO YOU COPE WITH THE STRAINS OF WORKING AND SINGLE-PARENTING?

Several years ago we wrote a book on single-parent families. We interviewed several divorced women who were trying to deal with the responsibilities of pursuing a career and raising children. When we asked them to describe their lives, the one word that they mentioned over and over again was "exhausting."

Divorced men experience similar feelings, primarily during those exhausting days when their children are visiting. When my son and daughter—ages 12 and 8—visited during the week, I would often leave work by 4:00 p.m. to be at home when they arrived from school. Then, I would cook dinner, eat with them and leave them doing homework while I went back to my office for a meeting. It was very tiring, but I simply had to accept it.

If your child is sick, you may need to stay home with her. And even in this era of men's and women's liberation, your boss or your colleagues may not entirely understand the reasons why you cannot come to work. Nevertheless, a very sick child needs the company of an adult to provide reassurance as well as support in case of an emergency.

Like many single Moms, a divorced father may find himself torn between the demands of his job and responsibilities to his children. In this conflict, it's important to strike the proper balance and always give your kids the attention they deserve. (See Letters section.)

LETTERS

Dear (teacher),

Thank you for meeting with me this morning as promised. Enclosed are stamped, self-addressed envelopes to send me any notices/reports you feel I should have. I very much want to support my daughter's education at elementary school. Thanks again and best wishes for a good school year.

Dear Doctor,

After phoning your office yesterday, I feel the need to express some thoughts I have concerning my involvement in my children's dental care.

As I am sure you can tell, I am a very involved father and have regularly attended the children's medical/dental appointments whenever possible. Since my divorce, I felt it even more important for me to be there as I am sure you can understand. Our interaction has always been positive and forthright and I am sure you've observed me as a caring and interested father.

As a medical professional, I sincerely hope you will work with me to simply keep me informed of scheduled appointments.

I'd appreciate a call when you get the chance. Thank you.

Dear (former wife),

I'm sorry you are unable to separate your feelings concerning me from acting in the best interests of the children. Your perception of me dominating physicians' visits for our children is not rooted in reality, and I'm sure you realize this at thoughtful times.

Certainly I have questions pertaining to our daughter's health at this time and understandably so. My questions to doctors are well thought out and sincere. They are not aggressive or out of hand as you implied in your phone call of this morning. I have never prevented you from asking questions you feel are important. I only wish you were willing to objectively discuss the children's health care without your continuing hostility. My behavior towards you is always polite and civil, even when you're raising your voice to me.

Dear (former wife),

Over the past weekend, I had the chance to think about our conversation concerning our daughter's medical problems. I appreciated your discussing your feelings and thoughts as well as listening to my suggestions. I only want to make the best possible decision for her—as we would do on any important issue concerning our children's lives.

I would appreciate knowing when you schedule our

daughter for her next appointment at the specialist so I can be there as well.

I also hope you will inform me of any meetings concerning the children as the school year unfolds. You don't even have to call me concerning dates and times—just drop me a short note.

CHAPTER VII

AS YOUR CHILDREN GROW

Studies show that divorce can have a substantial, long-term negative impact on children. But this effect can be substantially reduced if the non-custodial parent, usually the father, continues to play a meaningful role in their lives following the divorce. An essential building block of any successful parent-child relationship is open, honest communication on a variety of issues. This means that a divorced Dad must stay in close contact with his children so he knows what makes them "tick" and so they feel comfortable sharing their joys and problems with him. Effective communication also requires that you know how to carry on a meaningful dialogue with your kids, which includes speaking as well as listening. Dads must become proficient at selecting the best environment and the proper time for a constructive conversation, delivering their message clearly, using verbal and non-verbal skills to communicate their interest in what a child is saying, asking pertinent questions, and, perhaps most importantly, being non-judgmental.

During your child's adolescence, these practical abilities become especially important as you try to deal with a host of difficult issues. Chief among them is the natural rebelliousness which most teenagers exhibit as they attempt to separate themselves from their parents and establish their own identities. Adolescence is often a period of risk taking for young people, and this tendency may be exacerbated if a child harbors angry feelings toward you because of the divorce. A common form of risk taking is experimentation with drugs, alcohol and sex— some of the thorny problems which parents and teenagers must be able to confront openly. Here the example that you set for your children in your own personal life will have an enormous impact on how they conduct themselves.

Another issue that may arise for a divorced Dad is a request by your son or daughter to live with you. Children sometimes express this desire, particularly when they may be having serious disagreements with their mothers during adolescence, so you can't take it too seriously. But when this wish is made repeatedly, it may be time for action. A father should first determine if he wants to become a full-time single parent— a decision which will markedly alter your lifestyle. Then you must be prepared for a long, expensive process to change your custody agreement, especially if your ex-wife opposes this procedure, as many women often do. But the rewards of gaining custody can be great.

74. HOW CAN YOU COMMUNICATE WITH YOUR CHILDREN MORE EFFECTIVELY?

Over the years I've lost count of the number of letters and

postcards I've sent to my children when they were not with me on a visitation. Frequently the notes on them were extremely short and simple. I might write: "It's great receiving your letters. Can't wait to see you on Sunday." And I would draw a little sun underneath the words. Or I might say: "Hope you're having a great time at camp. How's horseback riding? Make any new friends? I look forward to seeing you soon." While the words were brief, the message to my kids was very powerful: "I miss you and care about you."

This is the message that must be delivered continually if you want to create a foundation for effective communication. It's more difficult for divorced Dads because you generally don't see your children on a daily basis as other fathers do. But, even when you're not with your kids, you can write them regularly so they know that you're always thinking about them. By staying in touch, you can communicate more easily with your kids during visitations. They will realize that you're always an important presence in their lives, and they'll want to talk with you about the issues that are on their minds. Even when they're not visiting you, they may call or come over to your home to discuss a problem. As one divorced father told us, he always knows when something is troubling his teenage son because he'll make an unannounced visit after school and hang around quietly until he's ready to talk.

This father has created an atmosphere in which his son feels comfortable talking. The boy knows that his Dad is there for him—not that he will always approve of whatever the boy has done, but that he will, at least, listen. (We'll talk more about becoming a better listener under the next question.)

Communication, of course, is a two-way process—speaking and listening. And in order to carry on an effective dialogue with your child, it's important to keep several things in mind.

1. Select the Proper Environment. Some children feel most comfortable talking while both of you are watching television or playing sports. Other kids prefer a quiet place where there are no distractions. It's essential to know your child well enough to recognize which environment is most conducive to a meaningful conversation.

2. Determine Your Main Message. As you listen to your child, think about what he's saying and how you feel about what he's saying as you formulate your own response. Both your thoughts and your feelings should comprise the main message of this response. Suppose your daughter is describing a problem she is having with a teacher who seems to be treating her unfairly. Perhaps you recall a similar incident that occurred when you where her age. As you empathize with your daughter, you also feel angry at the teacher for doing to her exactly what happened to you. But wait a minute! Is there more than one side to this story? Could your daughter be misinterpreting what the teacher is doing? Has she made similar complaints about other teachers? As all of these thoughts run through your mind, they will help you to decide on the message to deliver to your daughter. In this case, it may be that you should express your sincere understanding for her situation but also suggest that she should try talking to the teacher and resolving the problem that way.

3. KIS. These letters stand for Keep It Simple. The guiding principle of any communication is to make it as clear and simple as possible. If there are too many *ifs*, *ands* or *buts*, your listener will not fully understand what you mean. This same advice applies whether you're talking to a child or an audience full of Ph.D.s. That's the reason it's so essential to determine your main message before you begin speaking.

4. Know Your Audience. It almost goes without saying that you would present information differently to an eight-year-old than a teenager. But another element of effective communication is understanding how to deliver your main message in a way that will be most appealing to your child. Does he respond best to sports analogies, for example? Would an anecdote from your own childhood be effective? Your approach to a topic may be just as important as what you say about it. Knowing the proper approach comes, of course, from knowing your child.

5. Don't Forget Non-verbal Communication. Words deliver only part of the message. You can often say far more with non-verbal cues.

An arm around your child's shoulder or a hug, for example, communicates reassurance as the two of you try to solve a difficult problem together. Looking your child in the eye says that you're focused only on her when you speak, and that you're giving her your undivided attention when you listen to what she is saying. Facial expressions, like a smile or even an arched eyebrow, can also speak volumes when you're communicating with a child. They reinforce your message and give it much greater impact.

75. HOW CAN YOU BECOME A BETTER LISTENER?

Someone once said that humans are given only one mouth but two ears because we are expected to listen twice as much as we speak. Unfortunately, very few of us are ever taught how to be effective listeners. Here are a few simple guidelines.

1. Listen and Then Speak. How many times do you find yourself listening to your child and formulating a response before he has even finished speaking? Or even worse, jumping in and interrupting before your child stops talking? As a result, you may entirely miss the point of his communication. But whether you do or not, the message you've delivered is still the same: You care far more about what you want to say than what he is saying. This is often a sure way to shut down a real dialogue before it ever begins. Wait and hear your child out, then think about your response before you begin talking.

2. Ask Meaningful Questions. If you want your child to give you some significant information about what's going on in her life, don't ask questions that can easily be answered with one-word responses. For example, "How was school, today?" usually results in an answer like "great" or "lousy." If you want to elicit anything more from your kids, you need to ask questions that require more from them. For example, "What did you do in history class, today?" or "Tell me about the soccer game on Thursday." This opens the door for your children to provide a far meatier response.

3. Paraphrase What Your Child Says. This not only ensures that you understand what your child is saying but also communicates that you were listening. In addition, it may also give you some additional time to compose a response if the problem is especially difficult. You can use phrases such as "Let me see if I understand..." or "So what you're saying is...." or "It sounds to me like...."

4. Listening Involves Body Language. Non-verbal communication is just as important in listening as in speaking to communicate your interest and concern. Leaning toward your child, nodding while he is talking, smiling appropriately, and maintaining eye contact are all essential elements of body language. Eye contact may also assist you in interpreting your child's body language—reading between the lines—and figuring out what he is not telling you. This can enable you to formulate a far more effective response.

Even before she begins talking, your child's body language will often tell you if she is having a problem. You'll recognize it in the way she walks, how she holds her body, and the expressions on her face. This can be your cue to suggest to her that if she wants to tell you about something, you're happy to listen.

Of course, you must stay in close contact with your children so you know how to read the signs that they are giving you. We must emphasize again, as we have throughout this book, that you should see your children as often as possible—and communicate with them when they are not with you—in order to remain a meaningful presence in their lives.

5. Don't be judgmental. This advice applies whether you're speaking to your child or listening. Nothing is more detrimental to meaningful communication with your children when they have just told you about something they've done wrong than phrases, like: "That was stupid!" or "Won't you ever learn?" or "I'd have never done that!" This only makes them feel bad, increases their resistance to whatever you're going to say, and, even worse, insures that they will not want to talk to you about anything important in the future.

While your first response may be emotional, give yourself a few moments to think, rephrase what you're child has told you and ask them for further clarification. Then, try to work out a reasonable course of action together. Once you give a child the opportunity to tell you what's on his mind without the fear of being "put down," then he'll feel comfortable talking to you in the future.

> Once you give a child the opportunity to tell you what's on his mind without the fear or being "put down," then he'll feel comfortable talking to you in the future.

76. WHAT ARE SOME FACTORS AFFECTING THE LONG-TERM IMPACT OF DIVORCE ON CHILDREN?

Studies of the long-term impact of divorce on children focus on several key factors. First, and most important, there is the role of the custodial parent, who is usually the mother. Some women are successful in adapting to their new life as a single parent, which often involves handling the dual responsibilities of child rearing and employment. They can provide a stable home environment for their children, and a sense of continuity even though the traditional two-parent family has ended. This helps the children adjust to the divorce, feel relatively secure, and know that they are still loved regardless of the change in their family structure.

Some women, however, never seem to come to terms with the divorce. They remain bitter and angry toward their ex-husbands, and these emotions undermine the foundations of the home they are trying to create for their kids. The children may get caught in the middle of an ongoing battle that continues between their parents. And their mother may even try forcing them to take sides, which only increases their insecurity and unhappiness—feelings that may persist for many years.

Indeed, the second factor in the long-term impact of divorce is the relationship between the parents. As we have explained throughout this book, if parents can set aside their feelings about each other, at least when it comes to raising their children, then they can provide them with a meaningful family life. It will not be the same as the intact, two-parent family, but it will still give children much of what a family is supposed to give them.

The third factor in the impact of divorce is the role of the non-custodial parent, usually the father. According to a survey, about 40 percent of children in divorced families rarely if ever see their fathers. Some men, of course, were not very involved with their kids even before the divorce. For others, visitation becomes such a battleground with their ex-wives that they simply prefer to stay away. Still others try to run from their responsibilities for child support or alimony. And some men report that when their ex-wives remarry, they feel their role as a father has been taken over by someone else, so they drop out. Studies reveal, however, that these fathers are critically important to the long-term development of their children.

77. WHAT IS A CRITICAL ROLE THAT DI-VORCED DADS PLAY IN THE LONG-TERM DEVEL-OPMENT OF THEIR SONS? DAUGHTERS?

Experts have discovered that without a close relationship with their fathers boys experience a loss of self-esteem and self-confidence. Their performance in school may also suffer, research has shown . And if this problem continues, boys may eventually drop out. The failure to complete high school, of course, can dramatically affect their success in the working world.

Fathers give their sons important male companionship, a sense of security, and a feeling of being loved and valued for being themselves. Furthermore they provide their sons with essential male role models. Boys learn from their Dads what it means to be a man—how to hold down a job, how to conduct themselves on the athletic field, how to be a parent, how to relate to a woman. This knowledge is critical if a young boy is to some day become a responsible, well-adjusted adult.

Fathers, Daughters and Divorce. As children, girls often appear to adjust to divorce more easily than boys. They turn to friends for support and seem to resolve their feelings of anger, fear and resentment. While that may be true, don't be surprised if the feelings resurface. Studies now show that girls frequently remain angry at their parents long after the divorce occurs, and they especially resent a father who seldom comes to visit them. As girls enter adolescence and adulthood, the impact of the divorce may manifest itself in a young woman's reluctance to form a close relationship with a man, fearful that he will walk out on her just the way her father did.

Here again the role of the non-custodial father may prove critical in helping his daughter deal with these issues. A father who remains involved with his daughter can explain to her that not all relationships must end the way her parents' marriage did. He can provide a positive male role model, which will demonstrate that men can be caring, loving human beings, and mitigate her fears of forming intimate male-female relationships when she becomes an adult.

> **Boys learn from their Dads what it means to be a man.**

78. HOW DOES DIVORCE AFFECT YOUR CHILD'S ADOLESCENT REBELLION?

Adolescence is almost synonymous with rebellion, and most parents would do almost anything to avoid it. As social worker Maxine Varenko, who works with adolescents, told us: "This is a time in your children's development that they realize you're not the perfect human being they thought you were. Right up until about twelve or thirteen you manage to be up on a pedestal as a parent. Everything you said was taken as gospel...and it had to be right because you were Mom or you were Dad." Not any more.

Of course, this rebellion is a necessary process in your children's growth into adulthood. Children need to separate from their parents and establish their own identity. Frequently the custodial parent, which is usually your ex-wife, bears the brunt of this rebelliousness. She is the one who sets down the rules that govern your child's life most of the time. Don't be surprised if your children start complaining to you that your ex-wife is too strict with them and asking you to intercede with her to relax the rules. It may be extremely tempting to take your children's side against your former wife—especially if the two of you are extremely angry at each other—but this will not benefit your kids. It will only show them that they can play off one parent against the other to obtain what they want.

One divorced mother whom we interviewed told us that each time she tried to discipline her teenage daughter for not doing her homework, the girl would run to her father who imposed no rules on her at all. Eventually, the girl, who had been an outstanding student, began receiving only Cs and Ds at school. When the woman tried to talk to her daughter and deal with this problem, she would usually stomp out of the house and run to her father. This woman said she constantly felt like the overbearing parent in this situation.

Her ex-husband, on the other hand, could play a far easier role—the indulgent parent. Men often seem to think that they can take this position in the lives of their adolescent children. Since they only see their kids every other weekend, they don't have to live with the consequences of being too indulgent with them. That problem is often left to their ex-wives who must shoulder the ultimate responsibility for a child's well-being most of the week.

As we pointed out in the previous chapter, a consistent approach to your child's upbringing is essential for both parents. Otherwise the child might grow up without any of the self-discipline that is so critical for success. Ask yourself what would your ex-wife do in those specific situations that usually cause tension with teenagers—homework, chores, curfews, etc. If you have any doubt about her approach, or disagree with what she is doing, discuss the problem on the telephone. Or if you can't talk to each other easily, then discuss the issue in a letter.

The most important consideration is your children. They need the steadying influence of both their parents to avoid the excessive risk taking that often accompanies adolescence. Divorce sometimes exacerbates this risk taking and rebelliousness, as children take out their angry feelings and try to get back at you and your ex-wife for breaking up their two-parent family. So the need for a consistent, disciplined approach may be even more critical.

79. WHAT SHOULD YOU DO IF YOUR CHILD WANTS TO COME TO LIVE WITH YOU?

Don't do anything immediately. A child may express this wish more than once, especially during adolescence, if he is having a disagreement with his mother over a particular issue. However, if the child makes this request repeatedly and he is old enough—usually age twelve or older—so the courts will believe that he can carefully consider his own best interests, then it may be time to take his wishes seriously. (See Letters section.) As Maxine Varenko explains: "With boys, in particular, if they were young when the divorce went down, you find that their need to be validated by the man in the family could in fact be motivating them to want to make a change and to live with Dad for a few years."

It's important to explain to your child that this will not be an easy process (as we explain under the next question). His mother may oppose a change in the custody arrangement. As a result the child should expect to feel very uncomfortable in his mother's home. While openly asking to leave, he is still being forced to remain there while the custody issue is resolved, which can drag out over many months and involve some nasty battles between the contending parents and their lawyers.

> Changing the custody arrangement can be an extremely difficult and expensive process.

80. HOW CAN YOU CHANGE THE CUSTODY AR-RANGEMENT?

Changing a custody arrangement can be an extremely difficult and expensive process, especially if your ex-wife opposes it, as many of them do. You and your former spouse as well as the child may be required by the court to see a therapist for a lengthy period who will assess the current situation and then recommend whether you child's best interests will be served by remaining with your ex-wife or living with you. Remember, it could go either way so you must be prepared for any outcome. The court may also require that your child have an attorney, or you may decide that he needs one, so his wishes will be properly represented.

Suppose the therapist recommends a change in the cus-tody arrangement and the lawyer for your child also says that this is what he wants. The entire matter may be settled out of court, if your ex-wife is agreeable. If not, a trial will be neces-sary, which can prove extremely costly.

81. HOW SHOULD YOU DEAL WITH SEX AND YOUR TEENAGER?

Many parents find that discussing sex with their teenage son or daughter is extremely difficult. However, if you've developed a close relationship with your children over the years and they feel comfortable having a dialogue with you on a variety of issues, a discussion about sex will be somewhat easier.

Remember that actions speak far louder than words. Some divorced Dads decide that the time has come to "sow their wild oats" and they engage in a series of intimate relationships with a variety of women. This type of behavior sends the wrong message to your teenage children. Believe it or not, they do not really regard their Mom and Dad as sexual beings. They want their parents to be parents—safe moorings during the turbulent period of their adolescence. To see their father flaunting his sexuality, at the very time when they are trying to understand what it means to be a man or a woman, makes teenagers extremely uncomfortable. If the child resents his father because of the divorce, his blatantly sexual behavior may only increase these feelings of bitterness. In addition, a father, whether knowingly or not, sets an example by what he does that may be emulated by his children. So it's extremely important that this example be the right one.

A child who sees his Dad in a healthy relationship with a woman, one in which both people sincerely care about each other, share activities together and interact like a family, receives an entirely different message about the role of sex in human relations. This enables children to deal with their own sexuality much more positively, to treat members of the opposite sex with much greater respect, and to form more meaningful relationships.

It's important to make sure that your children are aware of the risks involved in sexual activity. And you must also decide whether or not to discuss the issue of birth control. These topics are much easier to discuss if your children feel comfortable talking with you, trust your judgment and respect the example that you've set for them.

82. HOW SHOULD YOU HANDLE YOUR TEENAGER'S RELATIONSHIPS?

Parents often worry that their children may spend time with peers who could lead them into trouble—teenagers who experiment with drugs and sex, for example. There is no way to prevent your children from being exposed to these things. You can only hope that your advice as well as the example you set will enable your child to make the right choices about them and about their friendships.

Since a divorced Dad is not with his children every day, don't expect that you can always have as much impact as fathers in many intact families. It simply may not be possible. Instead, you must face the fact that you have less control over the lives of your children. Therefore, it's important to carefully select those areas which you care about most deeply. Don't try to play the strict father with your teenager on every issue. After all, he can leave your home at the end of a weekend and pursue his own life until he sees you again. Pick your battles selectively; it's the best way to make a powerful impression on a teenager about the things that really matter to you.

83. WHAT ROLE SHOULD YOU PLAY IN FINANCING YOUR CHILD'S COLLEGE EDUCATION?

Most child support arrangements end when teenagers reach majority. And some divorced Dads believe that their responsibilities should end there, too. Unfortunately this may leave your children with no money for college, unless your ex-wife has a highly successful career or she has remarried and her husband agrees to pay for the children's higher education.

Suppose neither of these conditions exists, should you agree to finance your child's education? This seems fair if you have the money, but there is no reason why you should pay all of the bills by yourself. Your ex-wife should make a reasonable contribution, if she can. And an effort should be made to secure loans, scholarships or other financial aid. Perhaps the best way to deal with this situation—so your children aren't in jeopardy of reaching college age with no way to pay for an education—is to negotiate this issue at the time of your divorce. Agree with your ex-wife on a method to insure that your children will be able to afford college, and have it written into your agreement. You might use expenses at your state university (tuition, room, board, books, etc.) as the baseline for both parents' financial commitment to higher education.

If your ex-wife does not feel financially secure enough to discuss sharing college expenses at the time of your divorce, bring up the issue again after she is "settled" and try to agree on a fair approach to this issue. (See Letters section). The sooner an agreement can be reached, the earlier both of you can begin saving for your children's education to insure that the money will be there when they need it.

LETTERS

Dear (son),

I hope you feel as good and comfortable about living together as I do. Just hearing you around the house doing routine things makes me feel good inside. I love you very much and respect the very difficult decision you made to live with me. I just know we will do well together—as you will with your mother, seeing her frequently.

I know the past few months have been very hard for you. Let's hope your new routines will help you settle in and calm things down.

I look forward to seeing you tonight when I get home from work.

Dear (former wife),

I'd like to once again suggest what I proposed during the divorce period. This deals with the children's higher education and how we can equally pay for it. While you rejected any written commitments in the divorce agreement, I hope that by now you will re-consider. Since that time you have achieved much greater financial security.

I propose we each pay 50 percent of our son's higher education expenses and do the same for our daughter. This way both children know we are interested in their futures. It would be a big mistake to neglect this situation. Since neither of us can predict at this early date which child's education may cost more, this is the appropriate time to agree to equally share in both children's expenses.

I also propose that we have this agreement developed in written form so there is no question what will happen when each child starts college. Think this suggestion over. I know you will come to the conclusion that it's in the best interests of the children.

CHAPTER VIII

NEW RELATIONSHIPS

Whenever a divorced Dad develops a new relationship with a woman, it can have a profound impact on his children and their impression of him. Unfortunately, some men seem to go through multiple relationships following a divorce and decide to introduce each of these women to their children during visitations. Not surprisingly, a child can easily become confused and may even begin to resent his father for carrying on such a risque lifestyle.

Before you arrange for your kids to meet the new woman in your life, it's best to carefully evaluate the relationship and try to make sure that it really has some long-term potential. Of course, nothing is guaranteed; but if you wait a couple of months before introducing a woman to your kids, you might spare yourself the embarrassment of having to announce a short time later that this relationship didn't work out. Introductions should also be handled carefully or they can backfire on you. Instead of surprising your children by having the woman show up at the front door one afternoon, lay some groundwork with them over a couple of weeks by telling them as much as you can about her.

Then try to select an environment for the first meeting where everyone will feel comfortable.

For the relationship to be successful, both you and this woman must be able to balance your own needs against the needs of your children. This means dealing with issues such as sexual intimacy, enforcing discipline, and effectively defining her role in this new family.

Divorced Dads, of course, aren't the only ones to form new relationships; your ex-wife may have found someone else to share her life, too. For some men, this may be extremely painful, especially if they still harbored any hope of reconciling with their former wives and rebuilding their marriages. A man may also fear that his role as a father to his children will gradually be usurped by someone else. At this point, it's important to realize that no man can replace you in the eyes of your children, unless you let him. But remaining a committed father—on a part-time, non-custodial basis—isn't easy. It means creating a new family structure, one that may seem awkward and uncomfortable, at least at first. As a divorced Dad, you must deal with problems that don't confront other fathers—how to turn visitations into "high quality" time with your kids, for example, and how to stay in close touch with them during the days when they're away from you. That's the challenge of being a divorced father, but meeting that challenge can yield significant rewards.

> **For a new relationship to be successful, both of you need to be able to balance your own needs against the needs of your children.**

84. HOW SHOULD YOU EXPLAIN A NEW WOMAN IN YOUR LIFE TO YOUR CHILDREN?

The stereotype of a recently divorced man is someone who is too busy "sowing his wild oats", especially when it comes to sex, to think about anything else. Some men, of course, engage in a series of "one-night stands" that may continue for an extended period following their divorce. Many other men, however, feel very uncomfortable about beginning to date again after what may have been a lengthy hiatus covering the years when they were married and raising their children. A man often experiences extreme loneliness after his divorce and a longing to return to the way things used to be with his ex-wife and his family. As a result, some divorced fathers may find themselves "falling in love" with the very first woman who shows any interest in them and hoping to create a new home with her that will replace the one he left behind. The delighted Dad introduces this woman to his children, announces that they are planning to settle down together, and expects his kids to regard her as their new stepmother. Then a few weeks later, reality sets in. The disillusioned Dad has discovered some flaws in the woman of his dreams, he now has second thoughts about settling down with her, and she eventually disappears from his life...only to be replaced by someone else a short time later and the whole cycle begins again.

In an earlier chapter, we cautioned against making any major commitments or life changes in the weeks and months immediately following a divorce. You need an opportunity to decide who you are and what's really important to you. This advice is especially relevant when it comes to forming long-term relationships. Frequently, they don't prove to be lasting ones at all. And introducing a new woman to your children—or more likely a succession of new women—only confuses them and creates uncertainty in their lives.

When you begin dating someone, wait several months and make sure the relationship seems to be satisfying for both of you before discussing this woman with your children. Remember it may be difficult for them to adjust to the fact that there is a new woman in your life, especially if they still had hopes that you and their Mom might somehow get back together or if they are angry at you for leaving their home.

Once you decide to introduce the woman to your children, don't spring her on them suddenly and hold your breath to see how they react. This could be a recipe for disaster. Instead, over a period of several weeks let them know that you have met someone whom you care about and want them to meet during one of their visitations. You might describe the kind of work she does, provide some background on where she was born or went to school, explain that both of you enjoy many of the same activities, and emphasize that she would fit easily into the lifestyle that you and your children share together. Then, give them time to digest this information. Eventually, they'll begin asking questions about her and your answers will help them prepare to accept this woman as part of their lives.

We caution you not to compare this woman to your ex-wife. She is the children's mother and no one else should be expected to play that role. By trying to make an unfavorable comparison—no matter how subtly—between this new woman and your former wife, you only undermine her relationship with your kids. This also puts them in the middle and may even kindle their resentment toward you for leaving their Mom.

When you have finally selected the moment to introduce this woman to your children, it's usually a good idea to give them a little advance notice. Let them know a week ahead of time that they're going to meet her, so they can be prepared. Perhaps it's best to select a neutral setting for this first meeting—such as a restaurant or an amusement park—instead of having it in your home. In that way, the children won't think that she has already become a permanent part of your life—and your space—even before they've had a chance to meet her. If this initial encounter goes smoothly, then all of you might return to your home and spend more time together.

In the following weeks, you should certainly include this woman in more and more activities. Perhaps you could invite her to your daughter's softball game at school, as one man did. This was the child's environment and she felt comfortable getting to know her Dad's new friend in this milieu. But don't push any woman on your children too quickly. Observe their reactions to her and, above all, let them adjust to this person at their own pace.

85. WHAT SHOULD YOU DO IF THIS WOMAN AND YOUR CHILDREN DO NOT GET ALONG WELL?

This can be an extremely difficult problem for any man

because it can inevitably put you in conflict with the people you love most in the world. Perhaps something went wrong when the woman was initially introduced to your children. She may have been extremely nervous at meeting them or they may have been unprepared to accept the fact that you have a new relationship. Sometimes this problem will simply take time to be resolved— more discussions with your children, more meetings between the woman and them, more opportunity for them to become accustomed to her.

Under these circumstances, it's important that the new woman in your life values the relationship with your children just as much as you do. This is something that you should discuss with her before she ever meets them. If the woman is only interested in you and not your kids, then you may need to re-think your involvement with her. She may never try to fit in with your children, leaving you feeling continually torn between her and them. As a result, they may become increasingly angry at you. And if the relationship with this woman turns sour, you may become the loser all around—having lost her and severely damaged the relationship with your kids.

As a divorced father, you're no different from any parent. Your kids are a primary concern in almost every important decision that you confront. Sometimes it's easy to lose sight of this fact when you only see them every other weekend. Why shouldn't you be able to live your life any way you want? Because it can jeopardize your role as a father. For this reason, you may have to pass up some women who seem extremely attractive because they are simply incompatible with your responsibilities as a divorced Dad. While we don't pretend to believe that this decision will be easy for you, the alternative may be far worse.

86. WHAT ROLE SHOULD THIS WOMAN PLAY WITH YOUR CHILDREN?

As one woman told us, she just let the children "find their own comfort point with me." She tried to make sure they didn't perceive her as a threat to the relationship they had with their Dad or as an intruder in their lives. And she didn't try to become a surrogate mother. Instead, she was simply a caring, loving adult—someone who was happy to join the children in their activities, someone they could turn to for help when they needed it with school or their personal lives—and today, ten years later, they have accepted her as an integral member of their family. (See Letters section.)

Women in this situation must perform an especially difficult balancing act. Suppose a child misbehaves and his father is not around to see it. What should the woman do? Can she play the role of mother and discipline the child? Should she ignore the problem? Perhaps the best approach is for the woman to discuss the issue with the divorced Dad at a later time and let him handle it. My own significant other, for example, uses exactly this strategy and it seems to work very effectively. This enables her to help me in disciplining the kids without stepping in and acting like their parent. While I don't always follow her suggestions, at least I have the benefit of her advice and the final course of action is still left in my hands.

One woman told us that her position might have been much easier if the divorced Dad and his ex-wife had been able to communicate more smoothly. This would have enabled them to provide a consistent approach to child rearing and reduced the amount of tension that existed in the family. If battles break out over changes in visitation and custody, which sometimes occur after a divorce, these can also be very painful for a woman who may share the divorced Dad's anguish as he goes back to court to deal with his ex-wife. The best she can probably do is to give the man support as he copes with these problems.

87. HOW DO YOU STRIKE A BALANCE IN YOUR RELATIONSHIPS WITH A WOMAN & YOUR KIDS?

"I feel sometimes I can get lost in the picture," one woman told us, referring to the deep involvement of a divorced Dad—the man she loved—with the needs of his children. Fortunately, she realized, right from the beginning, how important this father's kids were to him. As we said before, a woman must be willing to make this commitment to your children—not just to you—or the relationship may become very unsatisfying for everyone. Otherwise she won't understand when you tell her that you need to spend some time alone with your kids during a visitation weekend. Nevertheless, a man must also recognize that a fulfilling relationship with any woman will require his commitment—his reassurance that he cares about her needs, does not take her for granted, and will not always expect her to take second place to his kids.

To strike a balance isn't easy. For example, suppose a man and woman who are currently living in different communities and have been dating for a couple of years finally decide to buy a house together. He wants a location that will enable him to remain near his job and his kids. But this will mean a seventy-five minute commute for her. At first, he is reluctant to move any farther away from his small children, fearful that they will feel insecure and he won't be able to reach them easily in case of an emergency. But eventually he realizes that this places too much of a burden on the woman. Finally, they arrive at a compromise— a house that takes him twenty minutes further from his kids but brings her closer to her job.

A man and woman must be prepared to discuss difficult issues like these whenever they arise. And if she also has children, the situation becomes even more complex. Then each adult has a set of important responsibilities which require both of them to demonstrate understanding and flexibility, to accept the fact that their quiet time together may be limited, and to make the best of it.

As adults try to juggle these relationships, parents or other relatives may prove to be extremely helpful. Sometimes they will volunteer to stay with the children for a weekend, so a man and woman can go away on a brief vacation. Even this brief respite enables them to catch their breaths, develop new perspectives, and perhaps most importantly, revitalize what they share together.

> **Your kids are a primary concern in almost every important decision you make.**

88. HOW DO YOU DEAL WITH SEXUAL INTIMACY AROUND YOUR CHILDREN?

Your children may feel uncomfortable, at first, knowing that you are engaged in a sexual relationship with someone other than their mother. However, they are far more likely to accept this aspect of your life when it occurs in the proper context. A couple of factors are important here. 1. The children often need time to become familiar with a new woman before she begins sleeping with you at your home. Once they accept her as someone who loves them, and they see that she also cares deeply about you, then it's much easier for them to adjust to the fact that both of you sleep in the same bed at night. But this will not happen immediately. In the meantime, some self control may be necessary. This may mean restricting your sexual activities to weekends or week nights when your children are not visiting. 2. Sex seems far more natural when a man and woman have a warm, loving relationship. If your kids see you regularly holding hands with this woman who has entered your life, kissing her on the cheek, putting your arms around her in front of them, they will realize that both of you share something that is very special. Sexual intimacy will then seem to be a logical element of it.

When you introduce this aspect of your relationship, however, may depend on the ages of the children. A young child, for example, may need more time to adjust to his father's sexual intimacy with another woman than a teenager for whom sex seems far more natural.

89. WHAT FEELINGS CAN YOU EXPECT TO EXPERIENCE IF YOUR EX-WIFE BECOMES INVOLVED WITH ANOTHER MAN OR REMARRIES?

One man we know was so elated when his ex-wife finally remarried many years after the divorce that he was telling all his friends about it. He had finally written his last alimony check, this gray-haired veteran of the divorce wars told us, and at last he could save some money for himself.

While some men may share this fellow's sense of relief, we expect that many of you may experience decidedly mixed feelings upon learning that your ex-wife has become involved with another man or even decided to marry him. One man we interviewed caught his wife in an affair, an incident which precipitated his divorce. Although profoundly hurt, he calmly walked away from his marriage and, for the sake of his children, still maintained civil relations with his ex-wife. But he spared no anger toward her lover and told us that if she ever decided to marry him he would never acknowledge the man as his children's stepfather.

Anger...hurt...sadness...these are only some of the reactions of divorced Dads who have been replaced by another man. In an earlier chapter, we explained how difficult it is for men to let go of the past following a divorce and face the fact that their marriage simply didn't work out the way they wanted. A man may even hope that he can turn back the clock, reconcile with his former wife, and resume their life together. For this reason, learning that she has become involved with someone else may be extremely hard to accept. It seems to slam the door on the past forever.

In these circumstances, a man may become highly over-wrought and even vindictive toward his ex-wife. He might begin making disparaging remarks about her in front of their children, or assume the role of "Grand Inquisitor" and question them incessantly concerning her activities. Of course, this type of behavior only hurts his kids, making them feel disloyal to their mother and probably resentful toward their Dad.

As hard as it may be, men must learn to put the past behind them and start to rebuild their lives after a divorce. This process takes time, certainly, and it's natural to feel that you're riding an emotional roller coaster while you try to adjust to all of the changes that are swirling around your head. But blaming your ex-wife and using your kids as weapons in the battle against her will only be counter-productive to your long-term relationship with them. And this should always remain your number one priority.

90. HOW DO YOU COPE WITH THE FEAR OF BEING DISPLACED IN YOUR CHILDREN'S LIVES BY ANOTHER MAN?

For many men, the anger and sadness at being replaced by another man in the affections of their ex-wives is accompanied by the fear that he will also replace them as the children's Dad. In some cases, this fear is entirely justified. One man told us that when his daughter developed a speech problem, he went to the doctor's office for a consultation. Upon arriving, he heard his ex-wife giving the doctor's secretary basic information about his daughter. Right in front of him, she stated that her new husband was the child's natural father. Weeks later, he discovered the same information was on the records of his daughter's pediatrician. Another man told us that when he went over to his former wife's house to pick up the children for their visitations, her "boyfriend"—a marine—would stand in the door with her and prevent him from seeing them.

Other divorced Dads have explained that they find themselves in competition with another man who may try to "buy" the affections of their children with expensive gifts. For a man who is burdened with substantial child support payments, this may be a financial foot race that he cannot possibly win.

Some men react to these circumstances by leaving the playing field. Since an ex-wife's new "boyfriend" or husband has far more access to the children than they do, divorced Dads often reason that they will inevitably be replaced in their children's lives, so what's the use of fighting it. The man retires from the field, licking the wounds to his male pride as both lover and father. Gradually he begins spending less and less time with his children. Eventually he may even be offered a job out of state and stops seeing them completely.

Unfortunately, these divorced Dads fail to realize that no one can replace them in their child's eyes if they want to prevent it from happening. But this result can only be achieved through perseverance, a determination to continually press your rights under the divorce agreement and custody arrangement, and a willingness to return to court, if necessary, to ensure that these documents are enforced.

Perhaps most importantly, it requires you to create a new family structure, one in which you've never functioned before and in which you have very little experience. For the non-custodial parent it means accepting the role of part-time father. This is an ambiguous position, at best, and most of us feel very uncomfortable with ambiguity. As a result, men often opt to abandon their children and begin a new family with another woman where they can feel like "normal" fathers again. But can they really forget the kids they leave behind? And what's the impact on them?

Like it or not, if you feel any commitment to your kids you must get used to being a divorced Dad. Instead of the regular routines that fathers pursue, you'll have to develop some new ones which will be unfamiliar and make you feel awkward, at least at first. You may even resent the fact that your time with the children will be limited—weekends, sleep-overs during the week, school vacations—but you must make the most of these days together. When you don't see the children, you'll be required to make an extra effort to stay in touch with them in ways that most other fathers never have to do—letters, postcards, telephone calls, etc. And even then you probably won't have the same impact on them as their custodial parent.

Finally, you may be forced to deal with some serious blows to your male ego when another man enters the scene and even occupies your place at the dinner table—a table that you bought in a house where you still pay the mortgage. What's more, your ex-wife may also wish that you would quietly disappear so that she and this new man in her life can raise your kids together. And there are days when disappearing will seem very easy.

But divorced Dads don't disappear, not if they really care about their children. It can be extremely painful to accept your role as a part-time parent and ex-husband, especially if you're trying to do it on your own. That's the reason we have suggested that you turn to friends and relatives to help you, or seek professional help from trained therapists, or support from Dads in a similar situation through the Divorced Men's Association in your state or other organizations that we list in the Appendix. Finally, a significant relationship with a woman, one who cares about you and your children, can enable you to create a more satisfying family life.

91. WHAT ATTITUDE SHOULD YOU HAVE TOWARD THIS NEW MAN IN YOUR WIFE'S LIFE?

Once I was having dinner with my children during a visitation and they asked me to stop making disparaging remarks about their stepfather because they felt badly about it. At that moment, I made a commitment not to repeat this behavior, and I have tried very hard never to break it.

While you probably can't be expected to develop a warm relationship with any man who comes into your ex-wife's life, constantly criticizing him in front of your children is also not very useful. Perhaps the best you can hope to accomplish is creating a distant, but business-like arrangement with him that allows you to communicate if the need arises. For example, your daughter may experience a flare-up from a past illness during a visitation. You need her medicine and call home, but your ex-wife is away and you must talk to her new husband. In this situation, it's essential for both of you to cooperate sufficiently so she can receive the medicine she requires.

Maintaining this type of relationship with your children's stepfather often requires enormous restraint on your part. It's another element of that new role you must create for yourself that we discussed under the last question. There's no direct benefit to you, only to your children. (See Letters section.)

LETTERS

Dear (former wife and husband),

I want to reinforce my willingness to meet with you concerning my suggestions for modifying the visitation schedule. It's a positive step and I'd like the chance to discuss the schedule with you. Let me know when it would be a good time to meet.

Dear (former wife and husband),

I'd like to stress my hopes that the children can be enrolled in a gymnastics class this summer. Please be assured that I am willing to share this cost with you. If their classes fall on days when the children are with me, I'd be willing to take them.

Please let me know your feelings on this matter.

Dear (daughter),

I'm so happy to hear you did so well on your swim test. Congratulations! It was great receiving your letter. J_____* is fine and we can't wait to see you next Sunday to pack for the trip. Have a wonderful second week at camp.

* Significant Other

Dear (son),

Even more than most years, J_____* and I enjoyed our Hanukkah with you and your sister last night. We realize how quickly time passes and how we need to focus on the many good times and experiences we have shared.

It's also good to see you excited and so positive about this year at school. I'm sure your strengths will enable you to be quite successful. I look forward to hearing from you soon. All the best.

*Significant Other

CHAPTER IX

IF ALL ELSE FAILS

Throughout this book, we have urged you to maintain civil relations with your ex-wife if for no other reason than to reduce the amount of tension on your children and make your visitations together as satisfying as possible. But what if this approach doesn't work, and your former wife seems intent on sabotaging your role as a divorced father—accusing you of withholding child support payments and trying to block your regular visitations? How can you deal with these problems?

In this chapter, we offer some answers.

92. IF YOUR EX-WIFE PREVENTS YOU FROM SEEING YOUR CHILDREN DURING VISITATIONS, SHOULD YOU EVER CONSIDER RUNNING OFF WITH THEM?

One man whom we interviewed was tempted to pursue this course of action. Fortunately, he changed his mind. The results would likely have been devastating, not only for the children but also for the divorced father. Being removed from their mother could have been terrifying for them. In addition, the man probably would have been caught and prosecuted, his kids returned to their mother, and his access to them severely reduced if not entirely eliminated.

93. CAN THE POLICE EVER ASSIST YOU IN ENFORCING YOUR VISITATION SCHEDULE?

The police generally prefer to stay out of these disputes, so they cannot be expected to help you significantly in having your visitation rights enforced.

94. SHOULD YOU EVER CONSIDER WITHHOLDING CHILD SUPPORT PAYMENTS?

Never. Your children have a right to receive this money for their support. And withholding it as a form of leverage to force your ex-wife to live up to the visitation agreement will only work to your disadvantage. If you ever decide to return to court, you're weakening the case against your ex-wife (as we explain in question 97) by refusing to make these payments. Earlier in the book, we also pointed out that Congress had passed legislation requiring non-custodial parents to pay child support. If they refuse, the money can be garnished from their paychecks.

Never withhold child support.

95. CAN THE AMOUNT OF CHILD SUPPORT YOU'RE PAYING EVER BE REDUCED?

Each state has established guidelines for child support payments keyed to a percentage of your income. If you lose your job or your income declines substantially for some other reason, speak to your attorney and ask his advice about whether you can have your payments reduced. Since the procedure takes time and requires a decision by the court, it can be fairly costly in attorney's fees. So you should not undertake this course of action, unless there appears to be a good chance of winning. In some cases, men are already paying the smallest amount of child support because their income is so low. Therefore, any change in their circumstances will probably not enable them to reduce the payments.

96. HOW ELSE CAN YOU APPEAL TO YOUR EX-WIFE TO RESOLVE THE CONFLICT BETWEEN YOU?

There are various approaches, each one involving increasing amounts of forcefulness. First, you might explain to your ex-wife that by taking out her anger on you, it only hurts the children. Unfortunately, this probably won't have much impact or she wouldn't be blocking your efforts to see the kids, in the first place. But, at least you will have fully satisfied yourself that "taking the high road" with your ex-wife doesn't work.

Next, you might try writing letters. In a letter, you can carefully state your rights as a divorced father and ask your ex-wife to comply with them. Sometimes a letter seems far less antagonizing than the sound of your voice or your presence at the front door. Your wife has time to read what you've written, vent any anger that she may experience, then calmly read your words again. In a quiet moment, she may realize that your requests are not unreasonable.

If this approach proves unsuccessful, then you must use the power of your divorce agreement which contains a specific visitation schedule. Every time she violates this agreement, you can report it to the appropriate local agency—such as the Family Services unit, for example—which will ask her to verify your allegation. It's important to take a firm stand on each violation, never allowing your ex-wife to have her own way on anything. While this may become extremely tiring for you—indeed some men find this process so exhausting and frustrating that they eventually walk away from their children—it's often the only way to keep your ex-wife "in line" and continue to see your kids. Once she knows that people in authority are watching her, she may be far less willing to risk violating the divorce agreement in the future.

Remember, your behavior must be exemplary, too. If you have neglected to pay child support—like so many men—you're not in a very strong position to be complaining about your ex-wife for not living up to her part of the divorce agreement. Make sure your own house is completely in order before you try to persuade some local authority to put pressure on your former spouse.

For some ex-wives, however, even this threat is not enough. Then you must be prepared to return to court to have your divorce agreement enforced. Of course, litigation will require the help of an attorney, which means significant expense. Naturally, men feel victimized by a system that requires them to pay more money to win what they had already won once before. But some divorces, unfortunately, seem to degenerate into a war of attrition and only by wearing down your ex-wife through a series of measures, like the ones outlined here, can you achieve any victories. This may require a financial "war chest", a high price but a necessary one to continue seeing your children.

97. WHAT CAN YOUR LAWYER DO TO ASSIST YOU?

Before involving your attorney, you should exhaust all the other options that we described in the previous question. Calling your lawyer for every aggravation you suffer at the hands of your ex-wife can rapidly make you *persona non grata*, while also proving to be extremely expensive.

When it becomes clear that your ex-wife will not listen to reason, then bring in your lawyer to forcefully protect your rights. First, ask him to contact your wife's attorney, apprise him of her violations of the divorce agreement and request that she comply with it. This may be enough to persuade her to let you see your children in accordance with the visitation agreement. If this approach proves unsuccessful, your lawyer must then file motions of contempt against your ex-wife and prepare for an appearance in court.

98. HOW CAN YOU HELP YOUR LAWYER WITH THE CASE?

Here are several suggestions.

1. Be as truthful with your attorney as possible regarding your ex-wife's actions and yours, as well. There's nothing to be gained by withholding essential information—no matter how damaging it may seem to your case—only to have your attorney discover it when he goes into court. That may be too late to adequately deal with it.

2. Keep careful records, including times and dates, regarding your wife's violations of the visitation schedule or any other part of the divorce agreement. Your lawyer will need this material to present a strong case in court.

3. Don't forget to tell your attorney if you have contacted any agencies connected with the court to inform them of your wife's behavior. Their records may also be helpful to your case.

4. Make sure you clearly explain to your lawyer what you want to accomplish. This will enable her to represent you satisfactorily.

5. If, for any reason, you believe that your attorney is not pressing your case strongly enough, discuss it with him and ask

for a thorough explanation of his approach. Should you still be unsatisfied, consider hiring another lawyer. You might seek a recommendation from a friend who has been recently divorced or talk to someone at your local chapter of the Divorced Men's Association.

99. SHOULD YOU REPRESENT YOURSELF IN COURT?

There are Do-It-Yourself Divorce Kits on the market for people who decide to represent themselves and save money. However, we do not recommend that you act as your own attorney on an issue as complex as fighting for your visitation rights. When the stakes are this high, you will probably be much better represented by a professional.

100. SHOULD YOU FILE FOR CUSTODY OF YOUR CHILDREN TO PUT LEVERAGE ON YOUR EX-WIFE?

Some men whose child support payments seem too high or who are denied access to their children by their ex-wives, will try to put pressure on them by filing for custody of their children. While this may appear to be an effective strategy, it does not serve the best interests of the children unless their father truly wants to become the custodial parent and believes he is capable of carrying out all the responsibilities connected with that role.

Otherwise, the children are simply being used as pawns in the divorce game. Throughout this book we have urged you to always put your kids first...this should be the primary goal of every divorced Dad.

APPENDIX A

RESOURCES FOR DIVORCED FATHERS

American Divorce Association of Men, 1519 S. Arlington Heights Road, Arlington Heights, IL 60005. (708) 364-1555. Offers divorce counseling and mediation for men as well as a list of attorney referrals and information for men who decide to represent themselves in divorce proceedings.

American Society of Separated and Divorced Men, 575 Keep Street, Elgin, IL 60120. (312) 695-2200. Helps men deal with issues such as unfair custody and visitation arrangements, alimony payments and property settlements, as well as safeguarding a man's right to remain actively involved with his children following a divorce.

Dads Against Discrimination, PO Box 8525, Portland, OR 97207. (503) 222-1111. Helps fathers to understand the legal aspects of divorce as well as offering information and support on family problems.

Fathers for Equal Rights, PO Box 010847, Flagler Station, Miami, FL 33101. (305) 895-6351. Assists men to protect their rights in child custody conflicts, provides information on the impact of absent fathers on their children, and researches the functioning of single parent families.

Fathers Rights and Equality Exchange, 701 Welch Rd., Ste. 323, Palo Alto, CA 94304. (415) 853-6877. Functions as an advocacy organization for fathers without custody of their children.

Parents Sharing Custody, 420 S. Beverly Dr., Ste. 100, Beverly Hills, CA 90212. (310) 286-9171. Provides information for divorced parents who wish to remain involved with their children and share the responsiblities of child rearing.

Parents Without Partners, 401 N. Michigan Ave., Chicago, IL 60611. (312) 644-6610. Regional and local groups are located throughout the country, assisting single parents deal with the problems of raising their children.

United Fathers of America, 595 The City Dr., Ste. 202, Orange, CA 92668. (714) 385-1002. Offers counseling and information for fathers involved in child custody disputes.

APPENDIX B

MARITAL HISTORY

1. Name
2. Address
3. Social Security Number
4. Birth
      a. when
      b. where
5. Health History
      a. Describe any mental and/or physical health problems which occurred during the past few years.
      b. Give details of any hospitalizations or extensive medical care during this time.
      c. Are you presently under a doctor's care? Why?
      d. Are you taking any prescription medicines?
      e. Do you have any health-related problems affecting your ability to work?
6. Education
      a. Give names and dates of schools attended.
      b. List degrees earned.
      c. List vocational skills or special certification.
      d. Do you have plans for additional schooling? If so, what do you intend to study?
      How long will you be enrolled?
      What is the estimated cost?
      What degree or certification do you expect to receive?
7. Employment
      a. Give name and address of your present employer.

b. How long have you been with this employer?

c. What is your job position or title?

d. What is your gross and net salary annually?

8. Real Estate

a. Address of the real estate.

b. What was the purchase price? date of purchase?

c. What was your down payment? Source?
Size of current mortgage?
Name of lender?

d. Itemize approximate cost of all major improvements to property since you purchased it.

e. Name of titleholder(s).

9. Marriage

a. Is this your first marriage?
If not, specify how and when previous marriage(s) ended.

b. Give place and date of this marriage.

c. Give name and date of birth of each child of each marriage.

d. Give address of most recent marital residence.

e. How long were you at this address?

f. Who left?

g. Date of separation.

h. Reason for separation.

10. Fault

a. Why do you believe the marriage is ending?

b. What conduct on the part of your spouse contributed to the breakdown of your marriage?

c. What conduct on your part contributed to the breakdown of your marriage?

d. Have there been any third parties involved? If so, please explain.

APPENDIX B

SAMPLE DIVORCE AGREEMENT
&
<u>JUDGMENT</u>

This action, by writ, and complain, claiming a dissolution of the marriage of the parties and other relief as on file, came to this Court on June ___, 19____ and thence to later dates when the Defendant appeared with counsel and the action was claimed to the Family Relations list and when the Plaintiff appeared to prosecute the claim for a dissolution of the marriage

The Court, having heard the evidence, finds the following:

1.   The Plaintiff, whose maiden name is _____, and the Defendant were intermarried on May ____, 19___.

2.   The Plaintiff has resided continuously in this State twelve months next before the date of the filing of the Complaint or next preceding the date of this decree, and all statutory stays have expired.

3.   The marriage of the parties has broken down irretrievably.

4.   There are three minor children issue of the marriage.

5.   No other minor children have been born to the Plaintiff wife since the date of marriage of the parties.

6.   The parties hereto have signed a written agreement dated December 1, 19__, concerning custody, child support, alimony and the disposition of their

property, which agreement the Court finds to be fair and equitable and which agreement has been incorporated into this Judgment of Dissolution.

WHEREUPON, it is adjudged that the marriage of the parties to this action be and it is hereby dissolved and there are each hereby declared to be single and unmarried.

AND, IT IS ORDERED, the Plaintiff and the Defendant shall share joint legal and physical custody of the three minor children. Each shall enjoy reasonable rights of visitation with the child or children when not in his or her physical custody.

a.   The parties shall share information about the children including, but not limited to, discipline, education, and non-emergency medical care.

b.   And, the parties shall participate in good faith open discussions concerning any major decisions affecting the health and general welfare of the children.

c.   In the event an impasse arises as to the issues related to access as set forth below, they shall, prior to bringing legal action, consult a third party whether clergyperson, family counselor or mediator, mutually agreed upon, in order to resolve the impasse.

d.   Every attempt shall be made to arrange for a mutually satisfactory access schedule so that the Defendant can continue to maintain an active role in the children's lives and maintain a meaningful relationship with the children. And, if either of them intends to leave the children with a babysitter, or day care provider, the other parent shall have the right of reasonable access during the time of the intended care.

e.   The parties shall share transportation of the children and they shall be free to arrange a mutually satisfactory schedule to effectuate this provision.

f.   In accordance with the parties current schedules, which does not allow for a specific access schedule, both parents shall have liberal access to the children. Given the parties present schedules, a specific access schedule is impossible so that the parties intend to operate under a flexible access schedule. In any event, unless other arrangements are made mutually between the parties, the parties shall share time with the children on the following holidays: New Year's Day, Easter, Memorial Day, Fourth of July, Labor Day, Thanksgiving, Christmas Eve and Christmas Day and any other legal holidays when the children have no school. Additionally, the parties shall share time during school vacations and summer vacations.

g.   The parties shall share time with the children on the children's birthdays. Mother's Day shall be spent with the Wife and Father's Day shall be spent with the Husband.

h.   Access to the children and time spent with the children shall be shared in such a way that each party maintains a close meaningful relationship with the children. The parties both express their love and affection for the children and each of them, individually and as parents collectively, desire to create an environment conducive to the children's best interest and one that adequately provides for their needs and welfare. Neither shall attempt to influence the children not to love or respect the other parent. Each parent shall work to express and promote goodwill towards the other parent and will not disparage nor permit any other person to disparage the other parent in front of the minor children.

i.   Each party shall keep the other party informed as to the whereabouts of the children, including an address and telephone number where the children may be reached while the children are in the other party's custody. If either party takes the children away from their home for any extended period of time the other party shall be informed.

j.   The parties shall make every attempt to communicate on a regular basis with the children concerning inter-family issues, and, from time to time, to consult with relevant counselors, if necessary, concerning those issues.

k.   Each party shall be entitled to speak with the children by telephone at reasonable times and intervals when the children are with the other parent. And, the children shall have free access to telephone either parent at any time.

        l.   The Plaintiff and Defendant shall both have the right to receive written reports from and/or have consultations with all health care providers regarding the health and well-being of the children. This shall include the children's doctors, medical and dental and psychological personnel, as well as any other person treating or consulting the children. The parties shall each have the right to communicate with and receive information, written and verbal, from all the children's teachers and educational personnel regarding the children's welfare and progress and shall be entitled to obtain copies of all reports prepared by school personnel concerning the children.

        m.   The foregoing is dependent on both parties' continued residence in the State and within close proximity to one another. The parties shall not permanently remove the children from the State without sixty days prior written notice to the other party.

        AND, the Defendant shall pay child support for the children in the amount of one hundred fifty seven dollars ($157.00) per week by way of immediate wage garnishment, to be paid in installment payments of three hundred fourteen dollars ($314.00) every two (2) weeks. Said support shall be paid until the youngest child, _____, reaches the age of eighteen (18). This support order deviates from the Guidelines based upon the shared legal and physical custody arrangement with the children with each party spending equal time with the children. Said obligation to pay child support commences on January 1, _____.

        AND, no alimony, lump sum or periodic, shall be awarded to either party.

        AND, the parties shall both maintain health insurance coverage for the benefit of the minor children as available through their places of employment and the parties shall divide evenly the cost of any and all uncovered/unreimbursed health related expenses incurred on behalf of the minor children.

        And, the Defendant shall be the primary health insurance provider and that the Plaintiff shall be secondary.

General Statutes Section 46b-84c, as amended, is hereby incorporated as follows:

(1) The signature of the custodial parent of the insured shall constitute a valid authorization to the insurer for the purposes of processing an insurance reimbursement payment to the provider of the medical services or to the custodial parent. (2) Neither parent shall prevent or interfere with the timely processing of any insurance reimbursement claim and (3) if the parent receiving an insurance reimbursement payment is not the parent who is paying the bill for the services of the medical provider, the parent receiving such insurance reimbursement shall promptly pay to the parent paying such bill any insurance reimbursement for such service. For the purposes of subdivision, (1) the custodial parent is responsible for providing the insurer with a certified copy of the order of dissolution of marriage or other order requiring maintenance of insurance for a minor child. Such insurer may thereafter rely on such order and is not responsible for inquiring as to the legal sufficiency of the order. The custodial parent shall be responsible for providing the insurer with a certified copy of any order which materially alters the provisions of the original order with respect to the maintenance of insurance for a minor child. If presented with an insurance reimbursement claim signed by the custodial parent, such insurer shall reimburse the provider of the medical services, if payment is to be made to such provider under the policy, or shall otherwise reimburse the custodial parent.

AND, each of the parties shall equally divide the cost of _____ school tuition, fees, books and other expenses until she attains the age of 18. In addition, the parties shall made their best efforts to equally share _____ college expenses. These expenses shall specifically include tuition, books, fees and other assessments. The parties' obligation shall not include room and board. The parties obligation shall be limited until _____ reached the age of twenty-one (21).

AND, the Defendant shall quit-claim to the Plaintiff all of his right, title and interest in and to the family residence. And, the Plaintiff shall thereafter assume and pay the first mortgage, taxes and insurance and household expenses relative to the family residence and the Plaintiff shall indemnify and hold the Defendant harmless therefrom.

The Defendant shall assume and pay the second mortgage until paid in full and the Defendant shall indemnify and hold the Plaintiff harmless therefrom. The Defendant shall vacate the residence within thirty (30) days of Judgment of dissolution.

AND, the Plaintiff shall quit-claim to the Defendant all of her right, title and interest in and to the family residence. And, the Defendant shall thereafter assume and pay the second mortgage on the family residence and other debt related to it and he shall indemnify and hold the Plaintiff harmless therefrom. In the event the Defendant sells the lot, he shall apply the net proceeds to the remaining second mortgage balance.

AND, the current value of the Defendant's salaried pension values on the date of dissolution shall be divided equally, and the Plaintiff's one-half share shall be paid to her by way of a Qualified Domestic Relations Order. The court shall retain jurisdiction to effectuate the same until such Qualified Domestic Relations Order is accepted by the Plan Administrator. The Defendant shall name the Plaintiff as survivor beneficiary on one-half (1/2) of any and all survivorship benefits available through said plan.

AND, the Plaintiff shall have no claim to the Defendant's Hourly Pension Plan.

AND, all IRA accounts shall be divided evenly between them.

AND, the Defendant shall have sole ownership and possession of the Honda motor vehicle and that the Plaintiff shall have sole ownership and possession of the Buick motor vehicle. And, each shall assume and pay any and all debt related to his or her motor vehicle and they shall each indemnify and hold the other harmless therefrom. And, each shall execute any and all documentation necessary to effectuate this provision.

AND, the personal property, including bank accounts, has been divided to the parties' mutual satisfaction.

AND, the Plaintiff and the Defendant shall each maintain their existing life insurance policies naming the minor children as equal irrevocable beneficiaries until the youngest reaches age eighteen (18). Both parties shall execute authorizations allowing the other party to check on the good standing of the policy from time to time.

AND, there shall be no order regarding the Parenting Education Program, Public Act 93-319. Neither party shall file any motions to modify custody or visitation rights unless that parent has completed this program or a similar program, absent emergency situation or circumstances are present.

UNIFORM VISITATION SCHEDULE

1.   Alternating weekends* from Friday at 6 p.m. to Sunday at 6 p.m.

2.   Alternating school vacations, Monday through Friday. (Christmas and

Easter schedules are separate.

3.   Christmas Vacation—Alternate years.

> Christmas Eve—10 a.m. to 9 p.m.
> Christmas Day—3 p.m. to December 27th at 3 p.m.
> Alternate Christmas vacations—December 27th, 3 p.m. to December 31, 3 p.m.

4.   Easter Vacation

Generally speaking there is a spring or Easter school vacation. Each year one parent shall have the 3-day weekend (Good Friday-Sunday) and the other parent shall have the balance of the Easter vacation, i.e. days off from school.

5.   <u>Alternate Holidays</u> (to coincide with alternate weekend schedule)

New Year's Day	Labor Day weekend
Martin Luther King	Columbus weekend
President's Day	Veterans' Day
Memorial Day weekend	Thanksgiving weekend
July 4th	

6.   <u>Mother's Day</u>—With Mother

7.   <u>Father's Day</u>—With Father

8.   <u>Summer Vacation</u>

Each parent shall have 2 unrestricted weeks of visitation during the summer. Each parent shall keep the other notified at least 30 days in advance of summer plans.

Each child shall have the right to attend summer camp (which may otherwise interfere with either parent's visitation).

*School vacation periods shall compliment regularly scheduled weekend visitation, e.g. begin or end so not to interfere with the other parent's visitation.

BIBLIOGRAPHY

Adler, Robert. *Sharing the Children: How to Resolve Custody Problems and Get on with Your Life*. Bethesda, M.D.: Adler and Adler, 1988.

Blades, Joan. *Family Mediation: Cooperative Divorce Settlement*. Englewood Cliffs, N.J.: Prentice-Hall, 1985.

Burgess, Jane K. *The Single-Again Man*. Lexington, M.A.: D.C. Heath, 1988.

Gardner, Richard A. *Child Custody Litigation: A Guide for Parents and Mental Health Professionals*. Cresskill, NJ: Creative Therapeutics, 1986.

_____. *The Parents' Book About Divorce*. N.Y.: Bantam, 1979.

Hill, Gerald A. *Divorced Father: Coping With Problems, Creating Solutions*. White Hall, V.A.: Betterway, 1989.

Krementz, Jill. *How It Feels When Parents Divorce*. N.Y.: Knopf, 1987.

Luepnitz, D.A. *Child Custody: A Study of Families After Divorce*. Lexington, M.A.: D.C. Heath, 1982.

Morgenbesser, M. and N. Nehls. *Joint Custody*. Chicago: Nelson-Hall, 1981.

Paris, Erna. *Stepfamilies: Making Them Work*. N.Y.: Avon, 1984.

Schaefer, Dan and Christine Lyons. *How Do We Tell the Children?* N.Y.: Newmarket Press, 1986.

Shepard, Morris and Gerald Goldman. *Divorced Dads.* Radnor, P.A.: Chilton Books, 1979.

Silver, Gerald A. and Myrna Silver. *Weekend Fathers.* L.A.: Stratford Press, 1981.

Wallerstein, Judith S. and Sandra Blakeslee. *Second Chances.* N.Y.: Ticknor and Fields, 1989.

Wallerstein, Judith S. and Joan Berlin Kelly. *Surviving the Breakup.* N.Y.: Basic Books, 1980.

ORDER FORM

To order more books from Blue Bird Publishing, use this handy order form. To receive a free catalog of all of the current titles (parenting, homeschooling, educational, relationships, and more), please send business size SASE to address below.

_____	*Divorced Dad's Handbook*	$12.95
_____	*Home Schools: An Alternative (3rd Ed)*	$11.95
_____	*Home Education Resource Guide (3rd E)*	$11.95
_____	*The Survival Guide to Step-Parenting*	$11.95
_____	*Road School*	$14.95
_____	*The O.J. Syndrome*	$11.95
_____	*Parent's Solution to a Problem Child*	$11.95
_____	*Dr. Christman's Learn-to-Read Book*	$15.95
_____	*Dragon-Slaying for Couples*	$14.95

Shipping charges: $2.50 for first book.
Add 50¢ for each additional book.
Total charges for books:_____
Total shipping charges:_____
TOTAL ENCLOSED:_____

NAME:_____
ADDRESS:_____
CITY, STATE, ZIP:_____
Telephone #:_____
For Credit card order,
  Card #:_____
Expiration Date:_____

Send mail order to:
BLUE BIRD PUBLISHING
1739 East Broadway #306
Tempe AZ 85282
(602) 968-4088 (602) 831-6063